A
REDNECK
REVERIE

A REDNECK REVERIE

The Rationale for the Trump Phenomenon

CLIFF OXFORD

Redwood Publishing, LLC

Printed in the United States of America
First Printing, 2020

Published By:
Redwood Publishing, LLC
Orange County, California
info@redwooddigitalpublishing.com
www.redwooddigitalpublishing.com

ISBN 978-1-952106-64-4 (hardcover)
ISBN 978-1-952106-10-1 (paperback)
ISBN 978-1-952106-11-8 (ebook)

Library of Congress Control Number: 2020915453

Book Design by: Redwood Publishing, LLC
Cover Design by: Graphique Designs, LLC

10 9 8 7 6 5 4 3 2 1

Dedicated to my older brother, Kenneth Lee Oxford

July 10, 1958 — November, 8 2008

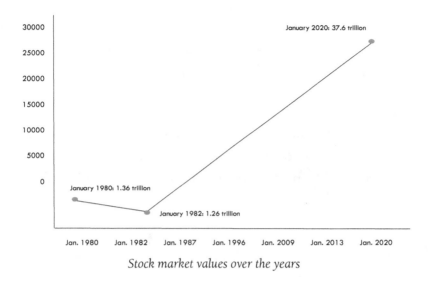

Stock market values over the years

"NAFTA was the final result of a process that began with Ronald Reagan in 1979. It had 14 years of effort and was central to North American progress. We are now in a different era. 23 years after that vote it is clear that a lot of our trade efforts are destructive."[1]
- Newt Gingrich

"I believe that NAFTA will create a million jobs in the first five years of its impact."[2]
- President Bill Clinton at a North American Free Trade Agreement (NAFTA) signing ceremony, Sept. 14, 1993

"Clinton's million-jobs figure was invented as a placeholder during the writing of his speech, to be replaced later by a more realistic number."[3]

- Michael Waldman, special assistant to the president for policy coordination, in his memoir *POTUS Speaks: Finding the Words That Defined the Clinton Presidency*

"[The figure is wrong] *due to a staff error.*"[4]

- Press secretary Dee Dee Myers to reporters after Sandy Berger, the deputy national security advisor, angrily notified Clinton of the mistake of the million-jobs figure

CONTENTS

PRELUDE

A note from the Publisher, Redwood Publishing:

In *A Redneck Reverie*, Cliff Oxford unravels the Trump phenomenon we've all seen unfold, while exposing his own vulnerabilities through his unvarnished personal Swamp Road to Wall Street story. This book allows its readers to see into the world of those who finally crested and created the landslide win and *why*.

Please note Cliff's personal story on Swamp Road is also at end of book in a final epilogue chapter we decided to call Personal Reveries—don't miss it. Added at the end, so as not to distract from the book's economic purpose; we catalogued these in vignettes, very similar to his breviloquent style as a columnist. It was a great compromise for Cliff, who wanted give everything had in explaining a complicated political process and me, who wants the reader to learn and enjoy a great read.

A note from the author, Cliff Oxford:

I have done my best to remember all events as they happened. While once in awhile, my sister and I will recall things slightly different, overwhelmingly we agree on much of the same. Everything I write about in this book—especially family events—are seared in my mind and *are* what happened. In a couple of cases, I might have changed a name if I thought the event would unfairly bring forth any type of negative light.

* * *

So, how did we get *here*—from country sunshine to community squalor? *Here* includes everything from holler to hood to Waycross and the biggest story is how Wall Street cashed in on making people poor.

So much of the hopelessness and sorrowfulness I see where rural communities have become economic ravines is similar to what I see when I drive down Memorial Drive in east Atlanta or all the way to San Bernardino, California, and headed in next five years to what I see in Skid Row in Downtown Los Angeles. Why? The common thread is both to get adoration at election time and then be abandoned as soon as the votes are counted.

My dream is for this book to heal the split votes so that neither can be written off by either party.

GLOSSARY

2.8M Renegade: A term used to identify a political subset of white, high-school educated, infrequent voters who appeared, seemingly from out of nowhere, to tip the scales in the 2016 election and could do the same in 2020.

affluent: Americans in top 20% of income distribution and most of the time politically engaged on retail political level of meetings and financial contributions to favor lower taxation.

elite: The super wealthy political donor class who drive the major decisions and policy outcomes in the United States.

elitism: A financial ideological coup that undermined and undercut working-class, middle-income wages to raise the fortunes of Wall Street at the expense of creating a wide swath of underclass in overall society.

holler: A ravine between mountains.

hood: A concentrated area of a city.

political proxy: A credible influencer, usually lucratively obligated to validate elite policy.

redneck:
red·neck | \ 'red-ˌnek \

1. sometimes disparaging: A white member of the rural laboring class.
2. often disparaging: A cultural meme for tawdry behavior, crude language, and simple opinions.
3. Me.

reverie: Longing for past; lost in one's thoughts or daydreams.

CHAPTER 1

You Don't Know Me, but You Don't Like Me

*"My own sympathy has always been with the
little fellow, the man without advantages."*
~ Harry S. Truman

AT DIFFERENT TIMES, Hollywood has hijacked the lifestyle of rural residents, from the pinelanderish family love of *The Waltons* to the depraved hillbilly characters of *Deliverance* to settling in a high-ratings sweet spot somewhere between a fun-loving, countryfied clan like *Duck Dynasty* and the tacky, bejeweled Mama June in *Here Comes Honey Boo Boo*. Loving the low cost of production, they consolidated the broad *country folk* under the label of *redneck*, framed as a subculture of uneducated, shifty, and shallow-minded white people. Unfortunately, it stuck. Redneck-labeled humor and hate sold seats, was easily understood, and brought big belly laughs with images of people whose dog lived under the house, who collected hubcaps and hung them on the front porch, and who proudly decorated front yards with "art." And with a shot or two of confederate flags waving in the background, rednecks and racism seemed to go together like rice and peas. The redneck label worked everywhere, including in the South, where people in places like Atlanta, Nashville, and Birmingham could join everyone else in laughing and poking fun at the life, times, and plight of poor white people. Folks in major media markets like New York City, Chicago, and Los Angeles got a free pass to laugh at a less-privileged class, with no purity tests or class prejudice taken. More like, if the shoe fits, wear it.

Not exactly fair, but not the biggest social injustice in the world. Then came Donald Trump defied the odds and polls to win the presidency. Stunned experts and pundits went looking for an electoral excuse and they found one: A big bump of 2.8 million white, high school educated, Renegade voters popped up in the rural precincts—the 2.8M Renegade. With that data bomb, and Trump carrying most of those same precincts with 70% to 80% of the vote, the experts and pundits leaned into the whole media image of rural residents as *rednecks* and *crazy country bumpkins* who won the election for Donald Trump, leaving them with one big question: *How could "they"*—meaning poor, white, uneducated people—*vote for this man?* And then they leaned harder—"redneck racism" was the only reasonable answer as to why this class of whites would vote for the man, Donald Trump, whose policies diametrically opposed their needs.

The experts then changed their labeled from the "dumb country voter" to the "low information voter." And that wrapped up the analysis of the election on why Trump won, ignoring some daring data that showed a direct correlation between higher turnout in those same rural precincts and the skyrocketing growth in suicide rates among white men.

Before those deaths, there was a track record of drugs and despair in the same population, which, until the 1990s, had lived up to Merle Haggard's #1 hit song "Okie from Muskogee." Its lyrics like, "A place where even squares can have a ball," "We don't take our trips on LSD," and "We like livin' right," screamed *clean country lifestyle*. But for last twenty years, there have been more overdoses on a per capita basis in my home region of South Georgia than there are in San Francisco, which, by the way, in Haggard's song was contrasted with the ideals of country life as being not "like the hippies out in San Francisco." In the fifty years since Merle Haggard and Roy Edward Burris wrote and released that song, the hippies have been doing very well; San Francisco is one of the most prosperous places on earth. The *Okies*? Not so much. Rural America has rotted. But why and how? That's what this book will reveal.

To say that Trump won because of redneck racism and country bumpkins is cute, like Honey Boo Boo, but it's not true. It also flies in the face of economics, history, and culture as much as the fantasy of John-Boy on *The Waltons* wearing fancy shoes in Southern summers during the Great Depression. I can't blame Earl Hamner, creator of the show, because he and CBS executives were selling the warmth of family love. But there is enough blame to go around for forty-five years of overlooking or simply ignoring one of the biggest stories of our time: An economic coup that pulled off a reverse redistribution of wealth from the working class to Wall Street.

It happened in broad daylight because of the redneck fantasy that was sold. Today, most people still don't understand the sentiment or situations in the rural areas of the US that make up 97% of the country's landmass. They don't know, sadly, that over the last forty-five years, dreams have withered by the wayside. And in all that despair, and now, commonly death, there starts to be a rationale for the Trump phenomenon, starting with how this destruction could happen to a corner leg of Americana. The rock-solid life of clean country living and a strong work ethic has now degraded into a world of jobless towns, meth labs, and little reason for living. In rural America, the bad guys took over. But it wasn't the kind of *terrorist bad guys* often depicted Hollywood-style. It was a form of financial terrorism designed to rapidly and unnaturally bleed out the economic blood from a vulnerable, mostly immobile, and, by-choice, apolitical group of citizens, sitting ducks if you will, to create unequal democracy where you get what you can buy, not what is fair or for the common good.

The policymakers in Washington, DC have chosen to ignore the dangerous, difficult, and unfortunate rural community rust because they are in what we call a tight spot—the elite donor class that created this economic downfall is the same group that funds their campaigns. With cash for campaigns through the money funnel of lobbyists, elites turned political parties into their political proxies. This is a chief reason why both houses of Congress and both parties refuse to address the basic questions—why and how an elite economic coup was given a free pass to pull the rug out from under tens of thousands of rural communities with three preplanned mile markers—the

Professional Air Traffic Controllers Organization (PATCO) strike, the North American Free Trade Agreement (NAFTA), and Opioids, Inc.

Having lived on both sides of the affected worlds, I differ from many academic scholars who have analyzed the situation. As someone who was raised in the swamp, a land where people are often written off and labeled as *redneck*, and yet also someone who walks and works with the elites of the world since leaving home, I am going to do my best to paint a true picture of and give an honest perspective on how these mile markers drowned the dreams and lives of family and friends back home and across all rural regions. In the pages ahead, I will kindly ask for your indulgence as I share the realities of being raised in *redneck country* as background in understanding the forty-five-year Wall Street wealth distribution strategy that allowed the elite to win big while a mostly immobile and apolitical group lost everything, including the spirit and pride of their souls. And those that lost big finally and belatedly, for their own good, voiced their disapproval by voting, in 2016, to put someone they rationally saw as one of their own into the highest position in the land. It's complicated, but I hope to answer the question: "How could they?"

My hope is that, with honest conversations and a better understanding of why 2.8 million Renegade voters—the 2.8M Renegade—who fell under the radar of pollsters but showed up, out of the blue, to vote for Trump, we can start fixing the big flaws caused by the Wall Street wealth retribution strategy. We can once again have competitive markets and prosperous communities. In short, no one should be ready to write off this part of our country—I'm certainly not. The venues that country folk love, like race tracks, all types of Gator Creeks, Waffle Houses, and jukebox bars, are just as influential to the American way of life as Broadway shows and Metropolitan Opera performances. As someone who visits and enjoys all of these venues and more, I've learned two things: 1) There are swamps no matter where you go, and 2) What you know is not based entirely on smarts, but also on where you're from and your exposure outside of that area. Keep that perspective front and center in your mind as you read the pages ahead.

I GREW UP in Ware County on Swamp Road, or "way out on Swamp Road" as people from our town, Waycross, Georgia, would put it. That was better than the put-down, "out in the sticks," which would have probably better described not only where we lived, but how we lived. Memories seep from my mind of coon hunts on Friday nights, homemade cane syrup and biscuits, fishing in Gator Creek, swimming in what we called "the watering hole" that Grandaddy dug out back for the cows to cool off in summer, family hell, redneck pride, the sounds of nearby railroad trains day and night, and cropping tobacco leaves, still sticky from the morning dew.

Sometimes, I wanted to run as far away from that swamp as I could. But I finally figured out that it's inside me, no matter where I lay my head. I was born and bred there, among people who were born from people who settled there because of the cheap boggy bay land and a simple desire to be left alone. But their luck and lifestyle ran out. Outsiders came. When I go home today, the only thing left is family hell, including my own, and a lot more of that than ever. Climate change brought repeated summer droughts and dried up Gator Creek and the watering hole; wildfires scarred the forests of the wildlife, and a financial virus from Wall Street sucked the soul and spirit out of the communities. Fast food replaced the cornbread and turnip greens, and suicides replaced most of the redneck pride.

It all started back on a summer evening in 1963 when the judge gave my daddy, Willie Clyde Oxford, permission to gain full custody of me, my older brother Kenny, and my sister Beth. He was to pick us up out of the Waycross "projects" where we were living with our barely twenty-year-old mother, provided he didn't hit her or have sex with her first. I was six months old at the time, my sister Beth was five, and my older brother Kenny was six. From there, we went straight to Swamp Road to live with him and our grandparents in the wood-frame house our Granddaddy had built from castoff railroad lumber. The workers would throw the lumber off the rail cars into a reject pile and Granddaddy would back up his truck and load up. The house was probably less than nine hundred square feet, but once a back room was added on, it was just a hair larger than a "shotgun house," called that because you could shoot a bullet straight from the back door out through the front. A hog-wire fence built around the house kept the billy goats at bay and out of Grandmama's flower beds that she planted around the front and back doorsteps.

Although I was too young to remember details of what happened that day, when I was a teen, my Aunt Shirley, Daddy's sister and Grandmama's youngest daughter, recalled to me the sad but circus-like arrival: Toby, Grandmama's yard dog who protected the chicken coop from the swamp foxes, ran out from under the house and leaped up on Beth and Kenny, causing them to cry hysterically for our mother. Grandmama came out with a broom to swoosh the dog away but nothing worked until Grandaddy kicked at him with his boot and muttered, "Git 'ut 'ere." The commotion set off the chickens, and that made the rooster start running around the yard. The pigs started squealing, too, because to them, the sound of a vehicle pulling into the yard meant they would soon have a trough full of slop, which Granddaddy collected every school day from Gilchrist Park Elementary school.

Even with the looming responsibility and complex mess of three children showing up on her doorstep to be raised, Grandmama accepted us without questions or conditions and never said one negative word to us about our mother. Grandmama's acts of kindness and love weighed positively heavy on Kenny, Beth, and me as we grew and was especially important during some dark times after our dad remarried five years later. But Grandmama was kind toward everyone; no matter the offense or situation, she was always there for the underdog, the accused, or whoever needed the most help. She was a doer, fixer, and pioneer who knew how "to make do," as she would say.

According to Aunt Shirley, the first night Grandmama took us in, she fed us a meal of cornbread, peas, and bacon, then bathed us and put us to bed. My baby food was smashed purple hull peas, which I still love today. The next morning, she told me, with a smile of relief, that Kenny and Beth woke up, ate breakfast, ran outside, and played. We didn't ask about our mother again until years later. But she was frank when she told me that Grandmama's biggest concern at the time was that I was still unable to sit up or pull up. Grandmama asked Aunt Shirley to drive her to Haines Grocery to buy a gallon of store-bought "sweet milk" for me to drink because she was afraid dairy from the milk cow would make me weaker.

Grandmama grew up the daughter of prairie farmers. Her motto: "Do it now or first thing in the morning." Once, just after Kenny had turned sixteen and started driving, he took Grandmama, Beth, and me to the drive-in theater to see a movie. We got home well after dark and were all standing on the back porch while Grandmama tried her normal method for unlocking the back door—she wiggled the key in the lock while pushing on the door. Unable to work her magic that night, she said, "Kenny you try it, bless kaydee." But Kenny didn't quite have Grandmama's touch, and broke the key off in the lock. So he just climbed through the back room window, and came around and opened the door. Before we went to bed, Grandmama told Kenny, "You'll have to go first thing in the morning and get a new key made at Frank Eldridge's hardware store." The next morning when we got up, Grandmama, already in her daily outfit—a fresh-pressed dress, every hair in place, and a gentle smile—had breakfast on the table and told Kenny, "Hurry up and eat, we gotta get that key made."

After we moved in, Daddy would be gone for days at a time on his job with the railroad. But with Grandmama always there for us, we stabilized into somewhat of an idyllic country life on 47.3 acres where we rode horses and goats and played with our large family of cousins who enjoyed coming to Grandmama's house out in the country. We walked barefoot to fish in Double Branches, an entry point into the Okefenokee Swamp. It was named by the Creek Indians who occupied the boggy, flat-and-wide pine tree landscape until the late 1880s, when Andrew Jackson's forces ran them out. That's when the Swampers like us took over, a lot of Scotch-Irish ramblers from the Appalachian region. When Daddy did come home from work, he was our hero and looked like the tallest man in the world.

We grew up cramped but safe in the house with two tiny bedrooms and a hallway that connected the kitchen, living room, and dining area with its sturdy table, "chester drawrs" (chest of drawers) and "chiffero" (chifforobe) bought for my grandmother by my Aunt Betty and Aunt Suzanne, my daddy's older sisters. There was a small gas space heater that we took turns at on cold school mornings, leaning up against it to warm our britches legs before running out to catch Bus 14, driven by Mr. Peacock who drove around picking up other swamp kids like us for nearly two more hours before dropping us all off at Memorial Drive School at 8:15 sharp. The Gilchrist Park school was much closer to Swamp Road, but it was the city school gerrymandered for segregation. I guess our hogs could eat their slop, but we unfortunately couldn't go to school there until 1994, when Waycross City Schools dropped its charter and was absorbed by Ware County.

Our house on Swamp Road had no air conditioning to keep us cool in the dog days of summers until I was in fifth grade. That's when my Uncle Jack, who was in the military and stationed in Texas, brought his family to stay with us for a vacation and Uncle Lennis, another one of Daddy's older brothers, drove over from Live Oak, Florida, and together they installed a window air-conditioning unit in the dining room window. *Almost like heaven* are the only words I can describe the first time I felt the breeze of re-conditioned air in the dining room. Even so, to this day, Beth, Kenny, and I declare that the house we still call home was the hottest place on earth in summer and the coldest place on earth in damp swamp winters, especially where we slept in the back bedroom. That room had been added on by Granddaddy and a jackleg carpenter, Audrey Albritton, along with a back porch that housed a picnic table and scales where we weighed the produce and grapes we sold from the fields and grapevines next to the house.

Our best playmates, the Stricklands, lived down the road and were considered well-off by Swamp Road standards. Mr. Strickland worked daily double shifts at the railroad shop, supporting his five children and five more nieces and nephews he and Mrs. Strickland adopted. They had a ranch-style home and a brand new car. One day, when Kenny was fifteen and I was nine, we were behind their house picking deer tongue, a wild medicinal grass dried and sold for malaria treatment and tobacco flavoring, when we saw them fill up two cars with suitcases. We dropped our half-full crocker sacks and ran over to see where they were headed. They told us they were going to Disney World in Orlando, about two hundred miles away from Waycross. It sounded like fun, but we had never heard of it. The Stricklands had what many people who come from where I lived dreamed of having: A tidy house on a concrete slab, a new Oldsmobile every few years, and enough money to have some fun and not worry about paying the light bill. The other dream people had was any kind of house, a four-wheel drive, three shotguns, a bass boat, and no worries about the light bill or how to pay for the next meal to feed the family. Although I'm sure few would have turned down a silver platter of money, for just about every soul where I come from, a good life is a simple one that includes a job, family, some fun, and being left alone.

FOR MANY PEOPLE in rural areas, those simple dreams are washed away today, which is largely the last best rationale for the phenomenon of voters who turned out to elect Donald Trump the forty-fifth president of the United States. But it wasn't an overnight decision—it was forty-five years in the making.

The last two generations have been sliding away from the Stricklands and toward the Beaches—a literally dirt-poor family who rented a shanty from local swamplord JC Lewis, about three hundred yards from Grandmama's house. The first time I stepped inside the Beaches' house around age eight, it scared me to be able to see the dirt on the ground through the spaces between the living room floorboards. I could smell the stench of the outhouse about twenty-five yards from their back door. They had pulled up stakes from Pennsylvania and come to Swamp Road where the dad had taken a job that paid just above minimum wage, around $1.60 back then. But the minimum wage is lower today than it was in the 1960s when adjusted for inflation, losing buying power just like most hourly wages for the past forty-five years. According to the Bureau of Labor Statistics consumer price index, prices in 2020 are 560.81% higher than average prices of goods in 1970. In other words, the purchasing power of $1.60 in 1970 would be equivalent to about $10.57 today. As I write this book, Georgia's minimum wage is $5.15 per hour, one of only two states that still have a minimum wage lower than the federal minimum of $7.25 per hour.[1]

When I go back and visit today, I no longer see outhouses and dirt through the floors. But there are very visible signs of a disaffected white underclass living in an elite-imposed economic malaise. Today, there are multiple generations living on top of each other—pretty much the same as us piled up in Grandmama's house—but now they are piled inside house trailers. Yet, there are a couple of distinct differences: The loss of life and the loss of hope. My Grandmama's house was always decorated with family pictures and doodads she bought in downtown Waycross at McCrory's and S.H. Kress & Co. five-and-dime stores. When you walked into Grandmama's house, you felt a touch of life. And on that day, when Daddy showed up with us in an all-out crisis, Grandmama had some good news—the Atlantic Coastline Railroad's extra-board had just called and wanted Daddy to report for work that evening. It was an on-call job with full benefits to cover other employees' absences, and while it was a great job to have, it left you living and dying waiting on the phone to ring. That call from work, to show up for a job, is the biggest thing missing from the squalid surroundings of the trailer parks today—and something that has been disappearing for the last forty-five years.

The first night of our stay at Grandmama's, Daddy left to report for work at 6:15 p.m. at the Waycross Rail Station, where he would board a train headed to High Springs, Florida. Also going to High Springs that night was the hope of his children going to college, hope of building a house, and hope of good health care. Yes, we had a family crisis, but we also had hope for a future.

CHAPTER 2

Killin' Time

AT THE TIME of our family crisis, President Kennedy was in office. As a Democrat, he had trounced the incumbent, Republican Vice President Richard Nixon, and carried the state of Georgia and our county, Ware, by more than 62% of the vote. Still intact in the South was the New Deal coalition, which was the grand platform of Franklin Roosevelt, who had basically made the working class a blood-like pledge: Vote Democrat, even if it's a yellow dog against a Republican, and the Democratic Party will make sure you have a job. That deal is important to remember when considering who executed the economic coup to take jobs away from the same working class, and to understand the results in the 2016 presidential election. Donald Trump won 70% of the vote in Ware County and ran the table in even higher numbers in counties considered "out in the country"—those rural regions, small towns, second-tier cities, and every other Renegade nook and cranny. That includes North, South, East, or West. And with very few exceptions, countable on one hand, this vast American landmass of wide-open communities has a common thread: a forty-five-year financial virus that is woven into their society as tight as ticks on skin. It's a crisis of disappearing living-wage jobs, chronic illness, opioid overdoses, and disappearing families. When I say families, I'm not talking about the political crutch of professed family values, I'm talking about the high rates of suicides and the societal unit known as "family" as a whole. Period. Dating opportunities declined in parallel with the loss of jobs, a little-known statistic that has gone unnoticed, but could be a big clue to Trump's election. No opportunities to build lasting relationships leads to fewer families, more loneliness, and more demotivation in the workforce.

The crisis has two gut-wrenching parts: 1) Forty-five straight years of declining wages, and 2) Increasingly higher prices for food and other necessities—an economic tornado that just keeps twisting on from one generation to the next. It changed the community fortune from a sliver of hope for the future, like Daddy had, to wide swaths of hopelessness—death by the day. It was a well-planned *economic coup* to redistribute wealth from growing, working, middle-class payroll wages to higher stock prices on Wall Street. As unemployment, high-school drop-out rates, suicides, drug overdoses, and home evictions have risen in that landmass of communities, stock prices and Wall Street as a whole have simultaneously surged: one surge indicating a gross decline in living standards, and the other, huge wealth increases and high returns. It was not a silent coup, or done in a backroom of a political convention, but it was sold out loud, like religion at an Elmer Gantry roadside revival, because getting the necessary votes to pass NAFTA was a full-court press in Congress. But finally, having the necessary votes, President Bill Clinton sat down at the signing ceremony and said, "I believe that NAFTA will create a million jobs in the first five years of its impact."[1] Wrong. Within two years, a financial meltdown and the collapse of the Peso evaporated any job gains in Mexico or the US, and by the third year, net job losses were close to 500,000 direct jobs. Data by the US Bureau of Labor Statistics reveal that 4.5 million US manufacturing jobs have been lost overall since NAFTA took effect.[2] These job-loss numbers do not take into consideration the community obligation chain job losses, which are those jobs that depend on people with other jobs. For instance, when factory workers use their wages to buy car insurance, movie tickets, and groceries, they support auto dealers, theaters, and stores in the local community. Workers no longer on a factory payroll, or left with jobs that only pay minimum wage, are forced to minimize or cease spending on those other businesses, leading to more layoffs.

The NAFTA con was no less cruel than if guns, tanks, and soldiers had marched in and scavenged the countryside like layers of carpet bombs from far above. Particularly vulgar was how Wall Street decided to make money off the people it made poor by bankrolling a new form of dollar-branded retail chains to fill the void of malls and stores closing due to the economic decline. The new dollar-retail economics has about the same financial returns—4.5 cash value profit—as predatory payday loans, pawn shops, and title stores. In other words, for every dollar spent, the elites want $4.50 back, or basically a 450% profit. And to accomplish that goal, they use the merchandising strategy of much lower quantity and quality for a little less money per ticket, but per-unit cost that is three to twelve times higher. That's what I discovered when I shopped at one of the dollar-brand stores versus Kroger, which itself is not exactly a low-cost leader like Walmart (see chart below). Why would someone pay $1 for two ounces of dish detergent instead of $1.25 for twenty-four ounces, or twelve times the amount? Because if that extra twenty-five cents were needed to buy the family or a child food for that day, you or I would make the same choice.

Predatory Merchandising

Product	Dollar Brand Store Price	Kroger Price	Comparison
Paper towels	$1 for 40 sheets	$1.25 for 96 sheets	100% higher
Dishwashing detergent	$1 for 2 oz. of Dawn	$1.99 for 24 oz. of Kroger brand	800% higher
Cash-back program when using a debit card	Maximum $50 for a $1 fee	Maximum $100 for $.50 fee	100% higher

Enough commentary and numbers. Let me paint you a real picture with real lives. Earlier I mentioned school Bus 14. Well, a childhood friend, Eugene Kicklighter, rode that bus, too. Eugene was smart as a whip with mechanics and machines, but scraped by in high school. His grades were just enough to graduate in 1980 and, soon after, he went to work in his dream job at the railroad. But before long, he was laid off. After that, he took a job driving a pulpwood truck, loading and unloading timber for $6 an hour—equivalent to a little over $10 an hour today—but he kept putting in applications all over the region for higher-paying jobs. Over time, he married and had kids, and now has grandkids. In the last thirty-five years, he has never really been unemployed because he hustled and stayed sober, but with the decline of industry in the region—followed by the loss of population—Eugene has not earned $100 per day since his first year out of high school when he worked for the railroad shops. More than once he had to settle for a job at $6 per hour, or less than $50 per day, just to stay employed. The coup screwed Eugene, a hardworking, sober, and honest person with simple dreams. Today, he has developed a limp and has diabetes, which he mostly neglects because he doesn't want to pay the office-visit deductibles. Still, he rarely misses a single day of work.

Starting with the Professional Air Traffic Controllers Organization (PATCO) strike in 1981, which occurred just a few months after Eugene graduated, the elite ideology was that people like him should never make $20 per hour because that spread between $20 and $8 per hour amounted to millions of dollars every day, which the elite determined could not co-exist with the returns Wall Street needs to keep afloat a big payroll and big returns on investments year after year. The money had to come from somewhere, and they found it. Forcing Eugene and others like him to work a lifetime at near impoverished wages created a financial ripple that crippled the next generation—two of Eugene's three children have suffered from substance addiction, relied heavily on food stamps, and are generally hopeless. When I saw one of them recently and asked how they were doing, their basic response was, "Nothing ain't happening around here." It's an accurate statement.

One summer in our early teens, Eugene and I proudly cut the grass at the Holiday Inn, but it has since left town. We took dates to the Green Frog Restaurant—gone. Prom dinners were at Bonanza—gone. Eugene, big as a bear, was a great wrestler and written up in the *Waycross Journal*—that newspaper is gone. When I asked Eugene's kids whether they shop at dollar-brand retail stores, they said, "Yea, we go there some, when we have to." In other words, when they don't have enough money to go to Walmart. Eugene rents a house outside the city limits in Manor, Georgia. All three kids live in trailer parks. That's today, but it's been a decline happening since NAFTA in 1994. Here is what they have witnessed since then:

- fresh produce grocery stores like Winn Dixie, Piggly Wiggly, and Big Star leaving like hobos in the night;
- dollar-branded retail stores flourish like mushrooms in a cow pasture;
- populations and incomes decline at the same time;
- high school dropout rates increase;
- personal bankruptcies increase;
- white male suicides skyrocket;
- life expectancy decrease;
- families killed by disease, drugs, and homicides from the economic wasteland.

Today, instead of my daddy going to High Springs with hope, as he did in July 1963, he would be going to work in fast food or at a local hotel where he would, at best, earn a smidgeon over minimum wage. He and Grandmama would have to apply for food stamps to feed us. Our family doctor, Dr. Porky Davis, would be miles away in Atlanta, not practicing nearby in Waycross. Major grocery chains Winn Dixie, Big Star, Pick 'n Save, and Piggly Wiggly would never put up stakes for a store.

Can you start to see some stark political rationale for a Trump vote?

Although I had watched the economic bleed-out in a drip-drop fashion since the early 1990s, I started this book and connected all the pieces together during the 2020 COVID-19 quarantine. When residents were required to stay in place, I was looking for something to do. I like being where the action is and I'm usually so wrapped in business, deals, and family that my plate runneth over. But COVID-19 not only gave me time, it also gave me clarity when I saw, in my own community, the aftermath horrors of an induced economic crisis.

Growing up in the swamp, I like a view of the water—so, in Atlanta, I live on the river that separates Sandy Springs and Buckhead, normally a supercharged business and entertainment district like no other east of New Orleans in the South. With COVID-19, suddenly time came to a crawl, and the sense of isolation and loss got very real, very fast. With Atlanta's Fulton County at an economic standstill—no restaurants open, no business meetings to hold, and no deals to close—I was looking for a place to fall apart.

I just started killin' time, as we say in the South when we can't find anything to do. I began by calling my family and friends who live in the Okefenokee Swamp where I grew up. Then, I expanded my reach and began to call folks all over the rural South—the area best known today as Trump Country. Whether I called my cousin Sonny in South Carolina or my friend Eugene in Georgia, I heard the same thing: *Nothing much has changed here, really; we're doing the same thing as we always do.*

COVID-19 had changed virtually *nothing* in most of the so-called Trump counties outside of Atlanta. Why? Because economic loss and isolation have been ingrained in their communities for the past forty-five years. At one point during the COVID quarantine, I drove to multiple grocery stores in a panicked search for tartar sauce, finally ending up at a dollar-brand store, twenty-six miles away. In places like Florence, Alabama, there are more than four hundred such stores within one hundred miles. That's because grocery stores with fresh produce left such rural towns in the South by the end of the 1990s. Yet here in Atlanta, and in places like San Francisco and New York City, people were shocked and appalled to see some half-empty shelves in the wake of COVID-19 hoarding.

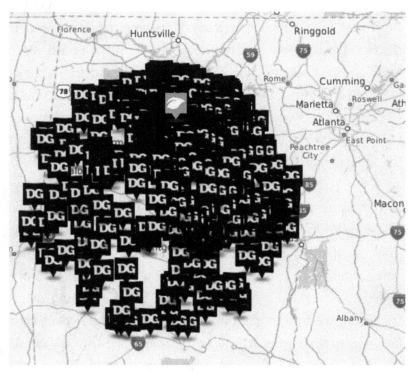

Data pulled from a dollar-brand store website store locator. Keep in mind that this is just one of the dollar-brand stores withing the 100-mile radius of rural Florence, Alabama.

Finally, instead of just killin' time, I started reading, researching, and thinking about the stark differences in COVID-induced lifestyle disruptions between the bigger cities and the rural areas. That led me to realize why Donald Trump, a reality-TV star, was elected president of the United States. In short, people like my friend Eugene had already been living in a COVID-like quarantine of economic despair for the past forty-five years.

The difference is that the standstill economics in Atlanta and across the US in 2020 were caused by a bio-virus—an unintentional act. In Trump Country, economic despair is the result of a premeditated wealth redistribution strategy to make China a low-cost US payroll powerhouse. It was a Wall Street economy bought and legally bribed. Call it flattening the economic curve to make more money for a few. The working-class wage earners were made to compete with people living in cardboard boxes. It was sold as a way to create more jobs, but instead left behind people who were mostly apolitical and far from upwardly mobile. It is fair to say that the people hurt the most lack what we might call, "the ambition gene," however, 2.8M Renegade voters ambitiously showed up out of nowhere, it seemed, as virtually every pollster missed them in the 2016 election when they elected Donald Trump president.

Less Than 1% Victories for Donald Trump

Donald Trump | Hillary Clinton		
Wisconsin	**Pennsylvania**	**Michigan**
Electoral vote: Trump 10 Clinton 0 **Percentage of votes:** Trump 47.22%, Clinton 46.45%	**Electoral vote:** Trump 20 Clinton 0 **Percentage of vote:** Trump 48.18% Clinton 47.46%	**Electoral vote:** Trump 16 Clinton 0 **Percentage of vote:** Trump 47.50% Clinton 47.27%
Source: https://en.wikipedia.org/wiki/2016_U nited_States_presidential_election_in _Wisconsin	**Source:** https://en.wikipedia.org/wiki/2016_ United_States_presidential_election_ in_Pennsylvania	**Source:** https://en.wikipedia.org/wiki/201 6_United_States_presidential_ele ction_in_Michigan

As you can see in this chart, without the 2.8M renegades, Trump would not have won any of these three areas.

Change in Reported Voting Totals – by Age, Race, and Hispanic Origin (2012 – 2016)		
Race and Hispanic-Origin	Change in Reported Voters	Change in Citizen Voting-Age Population
ALL AGES		
White non-Hispanic	2,808	1,588
Black non-Hispanic	-765	1,773
Other race non-Hispanic	1,051	2,284
Hispanic	1,494	3,333

In 2016, a large portion of the additional reported voters (2.8 million) were non-Hispanic whites who were also sixty-five years of age and older. The chart above shows all ages (from eighteen to sixty-five).

It is crystal clear that the surprise appearance of the 2.8M Renegade voters was the extra push to get Trump across the victory finish line in do-or-die states for both parties. Democrats still choose to ignore this reality. They are torn between the proclaimed "working-class party" and a dependency on donor-class elites funding their campaigns, especially at crunch time when one party has a run to overtake as majority in legislature, executive branches, and yes, now judicially all the way up to the Supreme Court. When the late Supreme Court Justice Antonin Scalia unexpectedly passed away, he was universally praised by both parties and all networks as a man with a profound legal mind. That's true and evident in his writings. However, virtually no one in cable, broadcast, or print news asked: *Why was a Supreme Court justice flying in with a 'friend' on a chartered jet to stay at a luxury hunting lodge filled with elites and owned by John Poindexter, the resort's super-elite donor class owner?* This was a Supreme Court justice and nobody even asked the question: *Who picked up the tab?* Believe me, I am not someone who buys into conspiracy theories; I don't give most of that stuff the time of day. I'm just giving this as one example of the vast power of the super-donor elite. If they want it, they get it. And they go both ways when turning political parties into proxies.

THE POLITICAL RATIONALE of Trump's Renegade voters would ultimately be no different than the rationale of the voters in the top-tier cities if economic despair were to set in for the long term. They would choose their own version of a Trump candidate to bring them back to economic life again, or at least have a fair shot at the life they longed for and loved. If nothing else, they would look for a candidate they thought at least had their backs. My guess, it would take less than five years, rather than the forty-five years it took to get Trump elected. As I write this book, many top-tier cities are large COVID-19 hotspots, and their residents are already looking for answers. Solutions now, not in forty-five years from now. The belatedness of the Trump vote is key to understanding the cultural blame the 2.8M Renegade bears in shunning civic participation. A planted economic virus encroached a very vulnerable population and wiped out its livelihoods. The working-class rural population was the only demographic to go down in both income and population numbers, the latter often contributed to suicides, much like that of the publisher of my hometown newspaper, the *Waycross Journal-Herald*. Facing a looming bankruptcy where forty-five years of economic decline had turned into decay, the publisher walked into his office in October 2018, put a gun to his head, and pulled the trigger, leaving behind a family publishing legacy of one hundred twenty-five years of pride.[3] But the forty-five years won.

After a few weeks in quarantine making those calls, I realized that anytime a human has no hope for tomorrow, it is like killin' time. And for the 2.8M Renegade, killin' time is killin' them—maybe for eternity.

IN HIS ARTICLE "No Sympathy for the Hillbilly," Frank Rich, columnist and commentator, wrote an article for the *New York Magazine* in which he, asked, "Why do they hate us?"[4] He wanted to know why so many white, working-class voters fell for what he sees as the antics of a con man and voted against the Democrats and Hillary Clinton. Why did they vote for Donald Trump, a billionaire whom Rich contends works against working-class voters with huge tax cuts for the rich while making cuts to health care and education, critical stepping stones for those who want to bootstrap themselves into a better future? Rich had some valid points but did not give an inkling of thought that the Trump vote was ultimately about accountability and results—the most rational vote of any—as I will try to show to the best of my ability and life experience.

By the way, I'll say it early on: I think these 2.8M Renegade voters could be up for grabs in the 2020 election. They are not yet a "sure thing" for a Trump second term; they are not that involved in the first place, unlike the evangelicals or gun supporters. And they are not benefiting from where we are today—low tax rates on super incomes, no taxes for highly profitable corporations, minimum wage suppression, trade deals with no labor or environmental standards—when a healthy majority of the American public opposes all of the above, including more than 40% of affluent Americans who actively participate in politics. Have you seen Nancy Pelosi go near Bernie Sanders or Alexandria Ocasio-Cortez (AOC), the progressive Democrat activist congresswoman from Brooklyn? The answer is no. She dismisses them as fast as she does the 2.8M Renegade. Bernie and AOC could have some real appeal to the 2.8M Renegade if they changed a cornerstone of how they communicate. For example, on one hand, we know white men have a long, sorry, steal-your-land-and-work-for-free track record of rigging the system—rightfully called white privilege.

But folks back home—with their diminished $8-per-hour job and squalor surroundings—say, *"White privilege my ass."* It's white, poor, and stabbed in the back.

The Federal Reserve Bank summarizes the economic hardship very well:

> *The white working class has declined in both size and relative well-being. Uniquely, among major socioeconomic groups the white working class decreased in absolute numbers and population share in recent decades. At the same time the five measures of well-being we tracked all deteriorated for the white working class relative to the overall population. The shares of all income earned and wealth owned by the white working class fell even faster than the population share.[5]*

The economic hopelessness is best explained by the Fed's last sentence: "The shares of all income earned and wealth owned by the white working class fell even faster than the population share." In the 2.8M Renegade's mind, all other groups are getting richer while the white, working-class male is getting poorer, which has disastrously dovetailed in with another already-mentioned trend: heck, they can't even get a date.

The rise of dating apps has made it much easier and faster to get turned down repeatedly. Together, it has become much harder for white men declining in status to find romance, build a relationship, and have a family. With the rise of social media, women have a full view and choices from the entire playing field, instead of having only a few men in close proximity to choose from.

An interesting Tinder experiment can be used to illustrate life for the rural white male in the real world.[6] The conclusion of that experiment was that 80% of the women on Tinder are chasing 20% of the most attractively profiled guys on Tinder, while the rest of the 80% of guys are chasing the bottom 20% of the women. What this means is that the dating market parallels the economic inequalities. The experiment, using the Gini index, measured the distribution of income among a population, and found that income was one of the chief drivers that caused women to swipe. Most (80%) are not looking for the richest guy, but they are looking for at least a HENRY (High Earner Not Rich Yet) as somewhat of a prerequisite, especially in hard-hit areas of job losses. The result is loneliness for 80% of white male populations and, according to scientific studies, loneliness hits men much harder than women.

In their 2009 book, *The Lonely American: Drifting Apart in the Twenty-first Century*, Jacqueline Olds and Richard Schwartz, a married couple, and both Harvard Medical School psychiatrists, observed it was more common for men than women to form closer bonds with their spouses at the expense of other social connections.[7] What if a male cannot find a spouse in the first place or cannot find a job to give him the funds for a relationship? He falls apart. Self-esteem shot. Before Tinder, a guy in a rural area might get rejected once or twice before finding a mate; now he can get rejected by thousands in an hour. On the other hand, if a guy swipes to show interest, the girl more than likely already has sixty to seventy people waiting to see her on the app.

We start to understand the rationalization between the rise of death and despair among white men and the rise of support for Donald Trump among the same demographic. The stats show the rise of deaths among whites are mostly among less educated white males, which is the same demographic that overwhelmingly supported Trump in 2016. If you dig deeper into the stats, there is a strong correlation between counties with high rates of despair deaths among less educated white males and votes for Trump. Some committed suicide as a way of solving their problems, others by doing drugs. Ultimately, their vote for Trump was because they saw him as a savior from the devil of their destruction.

Put yourself in the shoes of an average male in a dying town post-NAFTA. You are out of work, or holding a dead-end job for minimum wage pay, you haven't had a date in years, and the people who put you in this situation patronize you during every election with words and no action. Then those same people tell you that you are privileged based on your color and sex. You feel like you are under attack, and scientific research shows that any threat to self-esteem can lead a human being to increase their identification with a group or leader that offers support for your self-esteem. Trump ran a marketing campaign, referring to supporters as "forgotten" people who are "very, very smart," while Democrats offered lectures and purity tests on who could offend each other the least.

NAFTA, drugs, and diminished dating prospects created an environment ripe for a political entrepreneur like Donald

Trump and a black hole for those looking for an intellectual or academic answer. By the way, another great political entrepreneur was Nelson Mandela, who, when he took over South Africa, took great care to frame issues in such a way as not to alienate the white Afrikaner minority, which had ruled the country previously. When some of the radicals from his party tried to take cheap shots at the other side, such as taking rugby away from them as punishment, Mandela went against them and attended the games. Trump knows what he is doing when he eats a bucket of chicken and tweets about it.

The 2.8M Renegade is often accused of being a racist. Racism is a broad brush used to paint why this block of voters came out of the woodwork and selected Trump. But that's a sad story that flies in the face of the facts. If the 2.8M Renegades were absorbed in race politics, they would not have supported Barack Obama in 2008. It's true that they did not go back to the polls for Obama in 2012, but they stayed home and did not vote against him either.

When I asked several of my cousins in 2008 why they voted Democrat—for the first time in a long time—their honest answer was the same: "We hope a Black guy understands what we are going through." When I asked why they stayed home in 2012, all had the same answer: "Just another politician." If I pushed back with, "What about Obama's healthcare plan?," every one of them replied: "Cliff, I need a job." They are looking for that job that took Daddy to High Springs. The look in their eyes was that of a daydream about what used to be, instead of the nightmare they were living—losing incomes, population, and dignity.

CHAPTER 3

Loving Swamp and Holding Elites

SINCE LEAVING WAYCROSS, I've walked, worked, and slept with elites in their homes all over the world, yet I have never completely won them over. I think it's because I'm not one of them, and a lot of me never left the swamp—other than my time in higher education and a willingness to work around the clock in the world of the elite. However, while I find it's easy to forget the luxury and latitudes of the elite life, I will never forget what I learned from my grandmother and from growing up on Swamp Road.

Our grandmother, Myra Garrett Oxford, was born in 1901 in a family of seventeen children and had raised seven of her own before my brother, sister, and I arrived at her doorstep. She had come from a family considered well-off by Southern standards. Her father, Frank Garrett, at age seventeen, came up the Flint River with his new bride, the two of them riding one horse while he held the reins and led another horse that carried his mother, a full-blooded Cherokee Indian. The trio turned a cabin and forty acres into a one-thousand-acre, vertical farming operation with one of the biggest farmhouses in Georgia; they were well-to-do by the time Frank was forty.

Their oldest daughter, my grandmother, was striking, sturdy, and kind—just the type of temperament to fall for my grandfather, Willie C. Oxford, part of the Stribbling clan long known as dangerous outlaws who would warn people to *git off the land* before shooting them from the front porch. Out of that bunch, Grandaddy was six-foot-two and had the gift of gab and good looks to go along with it. But he turned out meaner than a cottonmouth water moccasin snake and even worse when he drank liquor, which he did—often. Before he turned forty, if he was breathing, he was drinking. But he also knew all there was about farming, welding, butchering, and farm animals, and if someone threw a dime in the air, he could hit it with a 22-rifle shot and be half drunk doing it.

Grandaddy had become a raging alcoholic during the Great Depression and ended up selling and losing almost everything he and Grandmama had accumulated earlier in their marriage. That included their house, which he sold to his first cousin for a beat-up Ford, a quart of liquor, and $250. He was as drunk as a skunk when he did it, and he did not tell my grandmother about it until after the deed was done. Later, they built the railroad timber house on Swamp Road on one hundred acres of land bought for my Grandmama by their son, Kenneth, who saved up his combat pay while he was serving in World War II. The only reason they kept the last 47.3 acres was that Grandmama was able to convince Grandaddy that they had already sold it off and were just renting it.

By the time we showed up on her wobbly, wooden back doorsteps—crying, confused, and hungry—Grandmama and Granddaddy were living mainly off the farm and his Social Security check of less than $262 per month. Still, because of her upbringing, Grandmama always had the poise of the well-to-do, but was equally comfortable riding with us on the bus to church or in Grandaddy's beat-up pickup truck to visit family and friends. Money and material did not seem to move her, but she always had high standards for the basic necessities—cleanliness, food quality, a positive outlook, and always one foot ahead of the next. She set the example for us to have.

That helps me feel justified in my belief that not all of the elites are driven only by greed. Most want to make a difference in the world and they see that they can do it with power and money. From the other side of the fence, I can also see that, in great contrast, the 2.8M Renegade re-engaged voters just want a job and to be left alone.

I confess that Wall Street's premeditated public policies to redistribute wealth helped me tremendously in my technology career and the company I formed after I left Waycross. While I think politicians like Presidents Barack Obama, George H.W. Bush, and Bill Clinton truly thought they could help the country in the long run. The truth is, they didn't. Long-term, they destroyed more than a job—it was generations of income, well-being, and livelihoods across more than ten thousand communities.

That said, Trump's election should not have come as a surprise. The vote for Trump should not be framed as just anger and rancor, nor can it be described in terms of a rebellion, because that would have meant marching the streets of the Capitol for change, as Dr. Martin Luther King Jr. did so brilliantly and nonviolently for equal race rights. Of course, many people say of these voters, "How could you believe Trump? He lies." The Renegade voter would respond, "Politicians have lied to me for more than forty years."

The vote for Trump was *long overdue*. For the 2.8 million typically apolitical voters, the Trump rationale was aspirational to more of a *reverie*, kind of like a daydream that one of them might actually be in charge of this country, filling them with the sense of pride they hold so dear and maybe even pulling them from the economic wreckage that they witness every day. It was about a return to their dream: *Work just enough, make a living wage, play more, and not care a rat's ass about public policy and politics.*

However, put all the cards on the table: Did their 2016 political rationale go beyond an aspirational reverie to some degree? Yes, it was also about accountability and, yes, payback to some degree. But the 2.8M Renegade voters also thought, *if all the media and Democrats are against Trump, then he must be for us.* By the time Trump came around as a candidate for president, the economic coup's three major mile markers had sunk into the souls of the communities and destroyed lives. Ultimately, these three mile markers would lead to the Trump runaway ramp for the 2.8M Renegade voters. Let me take a moment to quickly summarize the three mile markers. I will explain them more fully in upcoming chapters.

1. **Mile Marker 1: The Firing of Air Traffic Controllers.**
   When President Ronald Reagan dismissed over eleven thousand striking Professional Air Traffic Controllers Organization (PATCO) union members and then banned the fired employees from any future work for the government while PATCO leaders stayed silent, his actions and the unions' non-actions pleasantly surprised the Wall Street donor class.[1] The media bought and cast the "John Wayne story"—the president rode in on his horse and saved the town. The actual result was a forty-five-year decline of unions and worker wages.

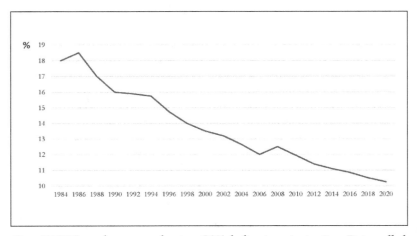

Since PATCO, we have seen about an 80% decline in unionization. Data pulled from Market Watch.[2]

2. **Mile Marker 2: NAFTA.** Eccentric billionaire entrepreneur and presidential candidate Ross Perot warned about the "giant sucking sound" of jobs that would leave the country if the North American Free

Trade Agreement (NAFTA) were put into effect.[3] But he missed one key point: That sucking sound was not only the sound of jobs being taken away, it was the souls and spirit of the communities. NAFTA undoubtedly created some higher-paying jobs for the upwardly educated mobile, but it also created wide swaths of vulnerability for people in rural and second-tier cities that were largely socially immobile. The local pain was far greater than any gain for the country as a whole. The elite lie to the 2.8M Renegade was that this economic change is good for you and nothing can be done about jobs leaving America. Thereby, people became poorer by the day. Around the year 2000, they could no longer afford to shop even at Walmart. Up sprang hundreds of dollar-branded retail stores—the only place to buy cheap "food" daily for many, but they were just another money-making investment for the same elite donor class who wrote and passed NAFTA. Yes, the elite made money off of making people poor.

3. **Mile Marker 3: The Addiction Crisis.** As the disease of hopelessness spread like spilt paint on a floor, the elite-backed pharmaceutical industry was eager to profit. The over-prescription of highly addictive pain medication was both a distraction and replacement for the soul of the communities that had been lost in a spiraling downward economy.

*Those three milestones led us barreling right to the final stop—**TRUMP IS ELECTED.***

BY THE WAY, the 2.8M Renegade pro-Trump voters for whom I will provide the rationale are not the people you see at his rallies. Surveys show the vast majority of people going to Trump events are middle-class voters, making between $50,000 and $100,000 per year.[4] They own the trailer parks—they don't live in them. However, the 2.8M Renegade voters are political nomads and punching way above their weight in determining the outcome of elections when they do vote. Do the math. If they give up and stay home, Trump's chance of losing rises above 80%. If they show up and vote for him again, his chances of winning are higher than 80%, if turnout is the same as 2016.

But getting real results for real lives is about moving beyond the rhetoric. To me, the first responsibility of the Democrats is to understand that the reverie is not about tax cuts, economics, and immigration policy. It's about a job, some fun and family, and being left alone. Politicians and pundits, as well as those who elect them, who write off all Trump supporters simply as ignorant, racists, and addicts, do so to avoid accountability for their own role in causing the climate capable of creating the Trump runaway ramp. But Democrats, count your blessings: If the 2.8M Renegade were not apolitical, they would have thrown out the working-class party long before Trump came along. It is only by exploring and understanding the 2.8M Renegade rationale for Trump that we can have both sides compete for the vote and earn it.

Yet, it's more than apparent that few people really understand the 2.8M Renegade. A *New York Daily News* columnist named Trump's voters, "bigots, bumpkins, and rednecks," and in the *New York Post*, they were referred to as "hillbilly class" and "white trash Americans."[5] If you look hard enough, I bet you could find some version of bigots and white prejudice among Hillary Clinton voters; and that was before she named a big part of the 2.8 million Renegade voters "deplorables." That comment alone might have been the deciding factor of the election, because that derogatory nickname motivated the 2.8M Renegade to take to the polls. Ironically, Bill Clinton's policy drove them from working class to despair, and then she named them to a new social class: "deplorables."

This book does not claim that this element does not exist, but it will show that the labels these people have been given are not the underlying rationale of the 2.8 million mostly high-school-educated voters who showed up for Trump in 2016. In fact, the data show that the last time there was a major bump in the same demographic—white, high-school-educated voters—was in President Obama's first election in 2008, where more of them voted for him than for Al Gore.

The disenfranchisement of the 2.8M Renegade did not happen overnight, and was not the result of a single presidential election. It was a forty-five-year long road of economic hell. And, as someone who has experienced the worlds of both the elites and the Renegades, I can clearly see how, on that journey, one side won big while the other lost everything.

GREENWICH, HOME OF the Wall Street elite, and Waycross, home of swamp road where I lived—even their names sound like oil and water. If you compare the total NAFTA wealth that has evaporated from the rural regions from 1994 to 2004, you will find it all adds up to the increase of wealth in Wall Street during the same time.

According to Pew Research, the timeframe from 1983 to 2001 saw an increase in wealth for all income tiers, but while lower-income families saw an increase of 67%, and middle-income families' wealth gained 42%, upper-income families saw their wealth increase by 85%.[6] The research states:

> The wealth gap between upper-income and lower- and middle-income families has grown wider this century. Upper-income families were the only income tier able to build on their wealth from 2001 to 2016, adding 33% at the median. On the other hand, middle-income families saw their median net worth shrink by 20% and lower-income families experienced a loss of 45%. As of 2016, upper-income families had 7.4 times as much wealth as middle-income families and 75 times as much wealth as

lower-income families. These ratios are up from 3.4 and 28 in 1983, respectively....

As with the distribution of aggregate income, the share of U.S. aggregate wealth held by upper-income families is on the rise. From 1983 to 2016, the share of aggregate wealth going to upper-income families increased from 60% to 79%. Meanwhile, the share held by middle-income families has been cut nearly in half, falling from 32% to 17%. Lower-income families had only 4% of aggregate wealth in 2016, down from 7% in 1983.[7]

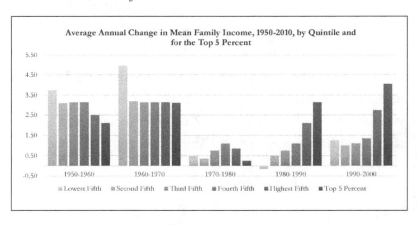

Average Annual Change in Mean Family Income, 1950-2010, by Quintile and for the Top 5 Percent

The gaps in income between upper-income and middle- and lower-income households are rising, and the share held by middle-income households is falling.

Share of U.S. Aggregate Income

Data pulled from Census and Pew Social Trends data.[8] [9]

In short, if you take a little bit of wealth from a lot of people—millions of people—it adds up to a lot of wealth for a few people. This reverse wealth distribution meant economically wiping out thousands of communities.

LET ME GIVE you a example of an equal level of NAFTA-like destruction on Wall Street: It would be equivalent to a carbon copy of the New York Stock Exchange in Thailand, and every trade would cost one penny versus $10 for every domestic trade on the New York stock market. On opening day, every US trader would trade in Thailand and bankrupt the New York Stock Exchange faster than a weekend fair.

There is enough blame to go around, and I'm not saying it was all Wall Street's fault, but it was Wall Street's plan. So while I will focus on the actions and consequences of the elite donor class who, due to privilege and power of money, create policy that rural Americans have little say over, those rural, Renegade voters take democracy for granted more than any other class of people, and their indifference have cost them everything. The communities like the one I was raised in are, by circumstance and choice, disturbingly insular. They have largely shunned civic participation or any worldly curiosity. It came as no surprise to me to learn that prior to 9/11, and its aftermath, back when Americans needed little more than a driver's license to travel between the US, Canada, and other locales in the Caribbean and South America, only some 15% of Americans and less than 2.5% from rural regions had a passport. That is why you still don't see many Renegades in Reykjavik or learning a romance language like French. In fact, you will be hard pressed to get them to go to a PTA meeting on a Monday night. Most would choose a job from 7 a.m. to 3:30 p.m., a smidgeon of overtime, a thirty-minute lunch break, and other than that, to be left the hell alone to live their lives. But while they are "smart, smart, smart people that don't have the big education," as Trump called them, they also don't have the sheer human population density to reinvent themselves if they could.

A Tale of Two Cities, Home Values				
Owner-occupied housing units (2017)	Greenwich town, Fairfield County, Connecticut 12,942 (population 2010)		Waycross City, Georgia 14,649 (population 2010)	
	14,874		2,782	
$20,000 to $49,999	0	0.0%	667	24.0%
$50,000 to $99,999	72	0.5%	1,022	36.7%
$100,000 to $149,999	106	0.7%	497	17.9%
$150,000 to $299,999	454	3.1%	199	7.2%
$300,000 to $499,999	957	6.4%	29	100.0%
$500,000 to $749,000	2,260	15.2%	0	0.0%
$750,000 to $999,999	1,940	13.0%	-	
$1,000,000 +	8,923	60.0%	-	-

Data for chart built from Social Explorer.[10]

Still, like the rural Renegade, the elites in Greenwich, Connecticut also have no desire to live outside of their subcultures. Even on the rare occasion when someone moves from a smaller city like Tuscaloosa, Alabama, they often do so only to relocate for work or school, and they're more likely to move to a town similar in scale and culture, like Allen, Texas. The folks in Greenwich vacation in the Hamptons, not down on the "Redneck Riviera" in Panama City, Florida—and vice versa. There's exclusivity to spare on both sides of the cultural divide. That sense of exclusivity is one reason Trump adversaries judge too quickly about the so-called country folk voters.

CHAPTER 4

Country Sunshine—"Livin' Like We Used to" Before the Coup

~

THE OKEFENOKEE SWAMP where I was raised is in a region known in folklore as being "below the gnat line" from middle Georgia—due south to the Florida state line, gnats and flying, needle-eye size stinging insects swarm the air and smother any open mouth, nose, or ears. From a geological perspective, the area is called "the fall line," a half-imaginary demarcation accented by a slight dent in the land, above which the piedmont climbs to the foothills of the Blue Ridge Mountains. "Below the fall line" separates the piedmont from the Atlantic coastal plains. There lies the Okefenokee Swamp, a crater on the ocean floor more than sixty-five million years ago. When the ocean receded, the depression filled with freshwater and wildlife of more than four hundred species of vertebrates, including over two hundred species of birds and sixty different species of reptiles. Grandmama's house was right on the edge of the swamp's basin bowl, saddling our house at night with complete darkness and sounds of the swamp's band of whippoorwills, bull frogs, and packs of hunting dogs on the weekend.

When the Swampers circled the land to set up homesteads into what had been Creek territory, the grounds were covered like well-made gravy—not too thick or too thin—with forests of longleaf pines. The trees were so well-spaced by their own nature that the longleaf tree limbs barely touched each other, giving off the perfect pitch of sunlight to see high in the sky. Forest historians estimated the longleaf pine trees at one time covered 85% of the southeast from Virginia to Florida and over eighty-five million acres. Today, fewer than ten thousand acres are virgin. Fewer than three hundred acres are within the swamp, only because neither man nor machine can reach them.

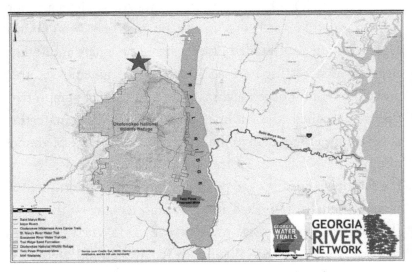

A map of the Georgia Swampland, with Swamp Road where the star is. Map courtesy of Rena Ann Peck, 404-395-6250, Georgia River Network.

Even though the longleaf pine was a majestic natural resource for our land, I had never heard of the species until I left home. Conservation of natural resources was not a big topic, even though we were growing up in a designated National Wildlife Refuge area of the Okefenokee Swamp. What we were familiar with were slash pine, which is basically a skinny, puny pine that can reproduce quickly and was planted by timber companies. Ever since the first Swampers showed up around 1858, the land was viewed as something not to be conserved, but used. It was a place where settlers carved out life by eating what they could shoot, catch, cut from, or grow on the sandy soil. Climate change and Mother Earth is not in the survival perspective. That's why Trump's tactics on climate change are not challenged, but cheered on by the folks in Trump Country.

The American moniker *redneck* has traveled down several roads of meaning: from coal miners who wore red handkerchiefs around their necks to avoid friendly fire during a union skirmish with mine and law enforcement officials, to Southern white laborers whose bare, sunburned necks contrasted with their lily-white skin covered by clothing. At first, the term "redneck" simply represented a class of working people who often wore white socks and drank Pabst Blue Ribbon beer. The movie *Deliverance*, with a cast of hillbilly characters, changed the *redneck* label for worse, to mean a crude, unkept, gutter class in any rural region from southern Alabama to Northern California. *Redneck* became the catch-all phrase to disparage hapless, flag-waving whites, replacing many other labels like *hillbilly, trailer trash, crackers, Okies*, and even *white trash*, which is older than any English slur except the N-word. Even rednecks started calling others rednecks *rednecks* if they were lower in economic or social class. *Redneck* represented a degenerate predator, a stereotype, and the only "politically correct" class caricature for wider audiences to laugh at.

However, a *redneck lifestyle*, not just the label, came back into vogue as incomes dropped in rural regions in the 1980s and 1990s. Singers like Toby Keith, and Gretchen Wilson with her mega hit, "Redneck Woman," made *redneck* a kind of cool, dark attitude of turpitude for Generation Xers like Donald Trump Jr., who said in an interview that he was a closet redneck because he enjoyed bow hunting.

IT WOULD BE a mistake to paint rednecks with such a broad brush when referring to those 2.8M Renegade voters who showed up in 2016. While studies have analyzed the psychological makeup of a Trump supporter, none have looked at the subculture of the 2.8M Renegade and their motivations for how they live their lives and, ultimately, why they got off their couches and drove down to their polling stations to elect the current occupant of the White House.[1] It isn't until their subculture influences are understood that we can rationally piece together what the last nearly-five decades have done to both drive them at one time deeper underground—and then to compel them back into action.

Setting aside some occasional macho talk, the 2.8M Renegade is actually pretty socially insecure; they're not particularly proud of their educational status, but smart enough to see how society treats someone in jeans and boots compared to what they call "a slick in a suit." This is not a criticism as much as it is to show they *do care* and *are smart enough* to see the class prejudices that they endure as no different than racial prejudice in their eyes.

The 2.8M Renegade has one tremendous weakness: a deep intolerance for anything different than themselves and their lifestyle. Does racism exist among the 2.8M Renegade? Yes, but no more than it exists anywhere in America. Non-whites living in a 2.8M Renegade community are accepted—as long as they share values and history. It was Southern rock bands like the Allman Brothers, in fact, who were among the first to desegregate music. But you can bet that African American Jai Johanny Johanson, drummer and a founding member of the Allman Brothers Band, dressed, ate, and talked just like all the other band members. It's not color that prejudices the 2.8M Renegade—it's *change*. It's change and anything that is different. And NAFTA brought a sea of change for this community. The 2.8M Renegade retreated deeper into their surroundings instead of looking for opportunity outside of that—until Donald Trump spoke to their status.

Today, they see Donald Trump as the person who can change America, instead of them changing to accommodate America. They would be happiest if the world would just stay static. They loved their status quo when they had a job and could be home by 4 p.m. And that is their silent reverie, as they say, "livin' like we used to"—*that's* why they voted for Donald Trump.

BUT WHY WOULD the 2.8M Renegade choose a reverie over a revolution for change? Because, historically, change is not a part of their makeup. A large part of the Swampers' ancestry came from Scotch-Irish settlers who first came to America in the 1630s to escape King George I who wanted them to join the Church of England. Instead of changing and backing the king, they crossed the Atlantic. This showcases their best and least desirable personality traits: loyalty to their culture and, if you don't leave them alone, defiance. Their skin complexion is pasty white and fair, while their minds are stubborn as a cold day is long.

Persistently unchanging is how they have always wanted their world to be, even to this day, if that means working as day laborers and millworkers and passing up college degrees generation after generation. They have no time or curiosity, for outsiders, or for anyone like myself who breaks fierce dedication to family and leaves the community they were born to instead of staying put forever. When I went off to college and came back home, my name changed from Cliff to "college boy." *You cannot change them.*

The story in the swamp is that most of its Scotch-Irish settlers came to America and first migrated to the Appalachian Mountains where the geography reminded them of their old homelands, then some of the rejects went south to take over the swampland from the Indians. Add some living off the land, going to church all day once per month, some sacred harp singing, and a little hell-raising, and you've got an early Southerner from the sticks. The Chesser family was one of the first known families to set up homestead in the 1850s on the edge of the swamp, close to where we lived. The father, W.T. Chesser, fled Liberty County after being suspected of shooting a land surveyor. By the way, the homes, grounds, and fields were immaculate, with every blade of grass cut short to keep out the snakes and mosquitos.

As you probably have noticed, the man the 2.8M Renegade elected has similar traits: Trump does not change his mind, he is resistant to new ideas, and he can often appear mean as a snake—and they love him for it. He portrays most of the attributes, which is exactly why the late Roger Ailes, chairman and CEO of Fox News, referred to him as an "uptown redneck."

TODAY, WHAT THE 2.8M Renegade's free time ultimately centers around, is television. Pastimes no longer include just country music and wrestling—those are pretty much mainstream now. But TV is a big part of life when you are mentally and physically remote like the 2.8M Renegade. Can you see the Trump connection? He knows TV maybe better than anyone in America now that Roger Ailes has passed. In fact, when I was in Roger's Ailes's office discussing my proposed and well-planned TV show about business, which had already been approved by Fox executives, he turned me down, saying that he wanted a viewer who watched 8.5 hours of TV per day and ate potato chips on the couch. Roger cut me down to size when he told me that nobody was going to watch my show because, "that's not what your rednecks watch; and businesspeople are too busy to watch it."

With the 2.8M Renegade, there is a dearth of exposure to culture outside of their own. Truth is, typically, the 2.8M Renegade shies away from books, magazines (other than *Field & Stream*), Broadway plays, art, music appreciation, and challenging conversation. Any social participation, in fact, is only likely to reinforce their narrow view of the world, not expand it. Growing up, I never heard one song of classical music, never knew New York City had an opera, and never visited the Grand Ole Opry, even though we loved country music. My brother Kenny and I played the song "Satin Sheets" until the eight-track tape broke. We'd watch every episode of *Hee Haw* and *Gunsmoke*, but we didn't read literature like *Moby Dick*, or know who great authors like Ernest Hemingway were, and Greek literature was foreign, we read *Old Yeller.*

AS WITH ANY tight-knit community, language is unique and reflective of a culture—and we spoke our Southern English as we pleased, with our own words: *minners* (minnows), *fur* (far), *I seen it* (saw), and *holler* (hollow) are just some of the cracker-speak that permeated my childhood. And from time to time, it still leaks out of me as it once did.

When companies relocate from the North to the South, they often do a media blitz with hokey Southernisms like "Hey y'all," "Ain't it great to be here," or "Fixin' to join ya'"—terrible PR because all it does is annoy Southerners. The first rule of making fun at the expense of a particular class is that you have to be one of them, and the second rule is that the fun-poking has to be taken as authentic. Yankees saying "ain't" and Mitt Romney saying "cheesy grits" instead of just "cheeze grits" (with a "z") is a sure sign of a fake, at least to the to 2.8M Renegade in the South. But Trump's pure crudeness is a match. And they like it in a New York accent because it is real and straightforward. By the way, in real *redneck* slang, it is not just one word but the string of words in a sentence that makes our hard-to-duplicate talk a grammatical quagmire, and a big reason why I think Professor Martha Saunders told me my third day in college, "I don't think you can make it unless you show up here at 5 p.m. every day for tutoring."

Below are some phrases she had to deal with in my Southern language.

- I am "fixin' ta" go to the store. The "ta" part is the dead ringer you know me.
- "This ain't nothing." We don't love "ain't," we love the double-negative with it and the all-time favorite is: "ain't got none." "This ain't nothing" is usually a setup for something that we describe as great.

No non-Southerner should ever try to speak the language because it also has so many sensitivities. For example:

- *Gread (d replaces t) day in the morning* or a putdown like *bit more than a man in the moon.* The "bit" word on the latter of these is the make-or-break word to accentuate the phrase. Someone who is not a Southerner saying "no more than a man in the moon" instead of "bit more" is a dead giveaway that you're trying to ridicule the language.

Here are some others: The enunciations below got giggles from my opponents and even team members in my first college debate when I said all three in my first delivery.

- A *glass of warter*, instead of *water.*
- *Lower the win-der,* instead of *window.*
- *Sal-man,* instead of *salmon* (pronounced sa-men).

We drop all consonants except where we should. In the word *salmon*, for instance, we make sure to pronounce that "L" loud and clear—we almost put two "Ls" in it … *sall*-man. And I still struggle today. I was recently eating at Driftwood Kitchen in Laguna Beach, California, and ordered sea "brim" instead of sea bream. The waiter politely corrected me.

If you don't talk like a 2.8M Renegade, you are at a serious disadvantage. Remember: They embrace everybody like them. If you try to mock the 2.8M Renegade, you will never get a second chance to communicate.

EMBRACING THE 2.8M Renegade means also knowing where they stand with religion. The 2.8M Renegade voters who got off the sofa are not the evangelicals and right wingers you see practicing religion on TV. The 2.8M don't go to church routinely because that's too much participation. They overwhelmingly believe in God because that's the only religion they know. They've never heard of atheism; to most of the 2.8M Renegades, atheism means you're probably talking about "the Arabs." So, Trump not going to church doesn't bother them—since they don't go to church. Trump says he believes in God, they believe in God. You start to see where we really have two peas in a pod.

CHAPTER 5

Mile Marker 1

When Push Comes to Shove— The PATCO Strike

~

"No one cares how much you know, until they know how much you care."

~ President Theodore Roosevelt

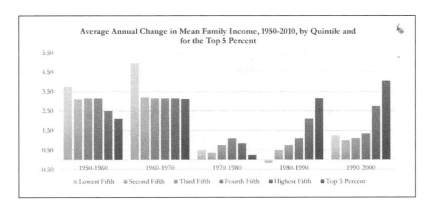

WHEN DID THE coup, or "the big screw" as I like to call it, actually start? You have to go back to a 1981 showdown. But to totally understand how the coup first smelled blood in the water and decided to launch the hit job on working class higher wages, start by remembering how Americans tuned in to blaring 24/7 televised cable news from December 22, 2018, to January 25, 2019, when the US federal government was shut down and government workers were sent home without pay.[1] Everybody was in an uproar, including an empathetic public. This was due to Congress' failure to pass funding legislation for its next fiscal year, attributed, in no small part, to a stalemate over the granting, by Congress, of the $5.7 billion demanded by the Trump administration for the border wall between the US and Mexico.

The government workers were furloughed without pay. Many TSA workers quit their jobs. Others called out sick in protest. There was little more they could do, despite the fact that many suggested they walk out *en masse*.[2] That happened only once before—back in 1981, when more than 12,000 members of the Professional Air Traffic Controllers Organization, or PATCO, went on strike against their employer, the Federal Aviation Administration.[3] And while that strike was poorly led, the lack of concern from the public and other unions sent a chill through organized labor for decades. In short, PATCO made unions the bad guys in free enterprise. Again, enough blame to go around. In the prior decade, unions had succeeded in increasing labor wages and benefits to the point where many unionized employees felt complacently secure to ask, "Why do we need a union?" Union leadership had had a steady trickle of scandals since the days of the Kennedy administration. In short, a perfect time for the first stage of an elite economic coup.

Back then, it was President Ronald Reagan who veered from every president since Franklin Delano Roosevelt on trying to balance the rights of workers and the rights of businesses to help grow the middle class. Reagan fired the air traffic controllers and basically rolled the union.

THE FAA-APPOINTED union employees of PATCO were in charge of making sure US air travel was safe and punctual, measuring the distance between every plane in American airspace and runways. These skilled workers manned the skies of America, performing highly specialized and high-pressure tasks—for which they would, from time to time, demand both shorter hours and wage increases through methods of deception and hubris.

Not that PATCO workers didn't pull their weight, both before and after joining the union. Some 80% of air traffic controllers were Vietnam veterans—many with a high school education and highly valuable government training.[4] They served long apprenticeships, only to make a starting salary of $20,000 a year. They worked up to two days, two nights, and one graveyard shift a week, and avoided collisions between airplanes that carried countless lives. Only after fifteen years on the job did a PATCO worker stand to earn an average of $33,000 a year—at a time when the average wage index was just over $12,500 annually.[5] It was brutally stressful work, and the union membership believed they deserved better compensation.

Knowing the airline industry's desire for on-time performance and aware that their status as federal employees made walkouts illegal, PATCO workers were prone to strong-arming their bosses through "slowdowns" (adhering to strict aircraft separation-spacing standards resulting in flight delays) and mass sick-outs as leverage against their government bosses. Their bosses, in turn, responded to these increased flights and PATCO demands by hiring more air traffic controllers and increasing salaries.

But by 1980, communications between PATCO and the FAA (which was staffed by appointees from then-president Jimmy Carter) had all but broken down. Airline deregulation in 1978 had led to free-market, *no frills* airlines jamming the skies, and the gas crisis of the late 1970s had left the cash-strapped airlines with little fiscal sympathy for the air traffic controllers who received salaries far lower than the pilots'—whom they considered their partners in the sky.

Seeking an endorsement from the nonetheless powerful union, GOP candidate Ronald Reagan courted PATCO's newly elected president, Robert Poli, in a letter in 1980, which stated in part:

> *I have been briefed by members of my staff as to the deplorable state of our nation's air traffic control system. They have told me that too few people working unreasonable hours with obsolete equipment has placed the nation's air travelers in unwarranted danger. In an area so clearly related to public policy, the Carter administration has failed to act responsibly.*
>
> *You can rest assured that if I am elected president, I will take whatever steps are necessary to provide our air traffic controllers with the most*

modern equipment available and to adjust staff levels and work days so that they are commensurate with achieving a maximum degree of public safety.

I pledge to you that my administration will work very closely with you to bring about a spirit of cooperation between the president and the air traffic controllers. Such harmony can and must exist if we are to restore the people's confidence in their government.[6]

PATCO CHOSE TO endorse Reagan over Carter, and in January 1981, Ronald Reagan took the oath of office. One month later, contract negotiations resumed. Citing safety concerns to a newly appointed head of the FAA, PATCO called for a reduced thirty-two-hour work week, a $10,000 pay increase for all air-traffic controllers, and better retirement benefits. In two short years, air traffic had increased 20%, and morale was unusually low. The FAA countered with an offer union president Poli deemed fair. Still, membership didn't find management's concessions to hours and working conditions acceptable. So, on August 3, 1981, more than 12,000 members of the air traffic controllers union failed to show up for work, leaving the FAA and the president to, in effect, fly the planes themselves.

Things might have ended better for the union—for all unions—had the membership chosen not to break the law. Had the PATCO strike resulted in airline fatalities, history might also view this walkout differently. But Reagan, like the air traffic controllers, called his opponent's bluff. Citing the statute in Title 5 of the US Code banning federal employees from striking, Reagan gave the PATCO membership forty-eight hours to either report back to work or be fired.

This was an unprecedented move in the history of government unionized labor. In the past, strikers weren't replaced, even when it was within the legal right of the company to do so. But until PATCO, no US president would dare make such a move against workers. Reagan changed that, dramatically, and it bled over to all union members, tragically.

Some of the striking workers quickly grew alarmed, and even as Reagan ordered military controllers and supervisors to commercial control towers, about 1,300 striking controllers returned to work. With flights quickly returning to normal and the strikers' position compromised, Reagan made good on his threat, and on August 5, more than 11,000 striking controllers were not only fired—they were banned from federal service for life. It could have been different if other unions had rallied behind the air traffic controllers. Across the board, the unions stood pat on PATCO.

The AFL-CIO, however, balked at the opportunity and forbade its union pilots, flight attendants, delivery drivers, and baggage handlers to honor the strike.[7] Likewise, consumers refused to back the striking workers. On the contrary, the media, consequently owned by big corporations, seemed to eagerly endorse the muscle of the movie-star president's cutting the union down to size. The media, being from the White House, was to play tough with organized labor everywhere and the management who employed them: The power of striking for better benefits, better working conditions, even a simple cost of living increase, came at the risk of one's job. The

White House had given industries nationwide permission to push back against its labor force, with extreme prejudice and profit, at the end of the picket. The elites smelled blood in the water, and this set up the idea of trade agreements without environmental and labor standards. They could run over the unions.

THE CALLOUSNESS OF the firing sent immediate shock waves among federal union workers everywhere. US postal workers, who had walked out on their jobs a decade earlier and were planning on voting down a pending contract at the time of the PATCO strike, accepted the terms instead. Where there had been thirty-nine work stoppages by federal workers in the twenty years prior to 1981—all equally illegal—such job actions ceased in the wake of Reagan's mass firings. Across the country, the word was out that public employees protested their working conditions at their peril—and all union employees were equally vulnerable.

In the public sector, corporations swiftly followed suit, clipping the wings of disgruntled labor with immediate dismissals and permanent replacements. From Phelps Dodge and the Arizona Copper Mine to International Paper and beyond, organized labor swiftly began to feel what my father had predicted: a "kneecapping."

But the impact of the PATCO firings was felt far beyond organized labor. For nonunion workers who toiled alongside their vested colleagues, any hope of collective bargaining came to an abrupt end. Over forty-eight hours, the solidarity of organized labor, on every assembly line, down every mineshaft, in every kitchen and classroom, and from coast to coast, had turned into a survival situation for each of those workers. They had lost the power of decades of solidarity and equality and now faced a new future with all presumed protections stripped away from the value placed upon the jobs that were supposed to be their livelihoods. Jobs, replacing their parents, on a line they'd taken over from their parents.

In the decades before PATCO, one could expect an average of three hundred major strikes each year. Twenty-five years after the air traffic controllers lost their jobs—for life—the number of actions by organized labor had dropped to some thirty per year. By 2020, less than 10% of American workers would belong to a union.[8]

IT WOULD BE naïve to believe PATCO alone contributed to the fiscal chasm that started to split apart under Ronald Reagan. The strike took place during the second of two recessions to hit America in as many years. The first taking place from January to July 1980, and the second, a more severe recession, went from July 1981 through November 1982. Before that, manufacturing employment was at its all-time peak (in June 1979). By the time PATCO workers went on strike, 1.4 million manufacturing jobs had been lost. The second recession cost another 2.3 million jobs, impacting a full 10% of the workforce—all at the same time the working-age population was growing by 21.5 million, and more women were entering the job market (a 6% increase over the decade).[9]

Even as factory jobs dropped from 23% to 18%, America's GNP remained steady over the decade at about 23%.[10] Part of this phenomenon can be attributed to the modernization of factories through computers and better machinery, which made output easier (even though automation also phased out many jobs in factories that were already downsizing as a result of the recessions).

The rise of automation through computers throughout the 1980s played a major role in the permanent shift in America from manufacturing to a service economy. Jobs in mining fell by nearly 6% and manufacturing by over 5% between 1979 and 1989, while service-producing industries rose by nearly 6%, with jobs in finance, insurance, health, and other general services like wholesale and retail trade all experienced growth over the same time period.[11]

It was in this climate that Reagan sent his chilling warning to the blue-collar world. The impact that the firing of the air traffic controllers of PATCO had could be seen on the labor force in towns like mine, and in other manufacturing and mining towns in 2.8M Renegade Country. With an increase in the labor force, a shortage of factory and manufacturing jobs, and employers battling recessions and their impact, America's labor unions, fearing recrimination and termination, actually agreed to wage and benefit *reductions*. This, together with more cost-effective production, helped keep industry afloat. Profitability improved, so much so that when the dollar weakened globally in the mid-1980s, manufacturing was ready to speed up export orders in addition to serving expanding markets at home—all for more hours, less pay, and fewer benefits.

AUGUST 20, 1982, was no ordinary Friday for Wall Street. Reagan's tax bill, intended to reduce interest rates and stimulate the economy, had been approved by Congress the day before, and the week ended with the Dow Jones index rising 10%, ushering in a bull market that would last nearly a decade. It's a prime example of why so many consider the 1980s the "greed is good" decade.

Reagan's tax cuts were designed to enable the elites to keep more of their money and created new classes of income called *yuppies* (young, urban professionals) and *dinks* (dual income no kids).[12] Upwards of 7.5% of middle-income workers actually transitioned to higher incomes over the decade. However, yuppies and dinks congregated around the larger cities and were a different breed than the 2.8M Renegade, who would get left behind in declining wages in the 1980s and jobs leaving the country in the 1990s.

The working middle class—8.5%—was losing income and falling into the working poor. A 1991 University of Michigan Panel Study of Income Dynamics (PSID) was a grim indicator that the middle class shrunk by a full 20% in that decade of "greed is good."[13]

While the widening gap between the rich and the poor should have been a wake-up call, the elites—after big wins on PATCO and one-sided tax cuts—decided to triple down. At the top of their agenda: NAFTA. NAFTA would become GOAT greed—greatest of all time greed.

While still only a presidential candidate, Ronald Reagan had proposed a common market for North America that would allow bilateral trade agreements among other nations to be expedited. Canadian Prime Minister Brian Mulroney got onboard with the idea, and by 1989, the Canada-United States Free Trade Agreement (CUSFTA) was in effect. Working with then president George H.W. Bush, Mexican President Carlos Salinas de Gortari sought to include his country in the liberalized trade plan, and by the time Bush left office in 1992, an agreement was drawn up between the three countries.

Ratification would be necessary, however, to enact the law that would doom what manufacturing jobs were left in America in the name of seamless trade and immense profit—and that was going to be a hard sell to the American people, especially those on the lower end of the widening fiscal divide. To that end, an invitation was extended to a young governor from Arkansas—the heart of Renegade country—to attend the Baden-Baden, Federal Republic of Germany meeting of the elite donor class behind the coup known as the Bilderberg Group (much more on this in Chapter 9).

Again, at the top of the group's agenda: NAFTA.

CHAPTER 6

Mile Marker 2

Give It Away—NAFTA

~

"People don't eat in the long run, they eat every day."
~ Harry Hopkins, advisor to Franklin Delano Roosevelt

IN 1992, WE were warned of a giant "sucking sound." Back then, a little over fifty-five million households had cable television and it was spreading like a wildfire —though it did not make it out on Swamp Road. Cable was a fast-growing entertainment outlet that had risen in news-stature just the year before when CNN, previously considered a news upstart, reported live from Iraq through the initial bombing campaign of the first Gulf War. Fewer than 23% of households had a computer in their home at the time, and the dial-up America Online service was a year old and available by subscription to PC users only.[1] Only eleven million people had cell phones, and people still tended to get their news from their local paper—in our case, the *Waycross Journal-Herald*, the publishing pride of South Georgia. Atlanta had two daily newspapers, *The Atlanta Journal* and *The Atlanta*

Constitution. By this time, the two newspapers were under one ownership, creating a monopoly that, according to Bill Clinton's political consultant, James Carville, set the news arc for the entire state.

At the time, Waycross was still reeling from the 1990 recession, which, by 1992, had the Ware County unemployment rate hovering at about 8%.[2] With that many people out of work in town, fast food became one of the more affordable options to feed yourself and your family in Waycross—especially when the increasingly laid-off population was being priced out of the healthier food options offered at the Winn-Dixie and Kroger. They were also among the few places in the area that were occasionally hiring. But independent restaurants like the Green Frog in Waycross, started in the 1930s by the Darden brothers who went on to found Red Lobster and Olive Garden, had closed and left town. By the way, the Dardens took another shot at Waycross in 2012 with a "synergy" Red Lobster and Olive Garden restaurant (which shared a kitchen), but closed those in less than a year after they discovered that opening one in Waycross was similar to opening one in Cuba—great idea but nobody there has money.

It was in this climate that America was presented with what was, at the time—at any time, really—an unusual presidential candidate: a plain-speaking, Independent Texas billionaire who rose to challenge the incumbent George H.W. Bush and Arkansas Governor Bill Clinton. With no political experience, but armed with a businessman's savvy and a knack for showmanship, Ross Perot used his own funds to buy up half-hour and hour-long prime-time TV slots—early "infomercials"—that he employed to connect directly with the American people. His moderate, fiscally conservative platform defied those of the status-quo candidates, warning against the growing influence of lobbyists and special interests in politics, and decrying the policy that dominated the political conversation: the North American Free Trade Agreement, or NAFTA. He was the first to call out the campaign contribution corruption on both parties, Democrat and Republican. Throughout October and up to the election, Americans tuned in over a half-dozen times to Perot's twangy, "Here's the deal" opening-line primers in economics—complete with low-tech charts and graphs propped up on easels and referenced by Perot, who always appeared seated at a desk. The shows were lecture-room caliber and invaluable to the electorate, but not the stuff the 2.8M Renegade reads every day. Some twelve to sixteen million people watched—and re-watched—programs with titles like "Chicken Feathers, Deep Voodoo and the American Dream," which warned that a Clinton presidency would result in Americans "plucking chickens for a living."[3] His message resonated with the electorate at large; one of his infomercials ran on the same night as a baseball playoff game and received a larger audience. Every 2.8M Renegade and rural worker in America should have not only watched the programs, but voted for him. But they didn't. Just like Bernie Sanders' campaign years later, Perot's candidacy required voter engagement and education—just the opposite of what the 2.8M Renegade wants. Not interested. Most would prefer a benevolent dictator who would lead them along, as long as they could have a job where they could have a shotgun, a family, and a four-wheel drive.

During one of the presidential debates, the media cast Perot as an alarmist when he said:

> *Everybody's nibbling around the edges. Let's go to the center of the bulls-eye, the core problem. And believe me, everybody on the factory floor all over this country knows it. You implement that NAFTA, the Mexican trade agreement, where they pay people a dollar an hour, have no health care, no retirement, no pollution controls, et cetera, et cetera, et cetera, and you're going to hear a giant sucking sound of jobs being pulled out of this country right at a time when we need the tax base to pay the debt and pay down the interest on the debt and get our house back in order.*[4]

The Republican and Democratic establishments (Bilderberg elites) played tricks to make Perot look like an eccentric fool. They had people crash his daughter's wedding, and when Perot went on TV to complain, they made him look like he was bombastic. Years later, they would do the same thing to Michael Bloomberg to squash his candidacy before it started, making out that he was a serial sexual harasser. The elites can put up with a Biden or Trump, they can't allow a true independent like Bloomberg or Perot to get elected.

However, in the end, as a third-party candidate, Perot would capture an impressive 18.9% of the popular vote, though he failed to capture a single state.[5] But by the time of his death in 2019, he was eulogized as a pioneer of political media, and a prophet about NAFTA. In short, if Perot had been elected, there would have been no NAFTA, far fewer meth mouths in the South, and the Dow never would have seen 20,000.

"THE BIG SCREW" officially started after the NAFTA bill passed the senate on November 20, 1993, 61–38, two days shy of the thirty-year anniversary of President John F. Kennedy's assassination, and just a few months shy of that day, thirty years earlier, when my daddy caught the train to High Springs, Florida. Speaker Newt Gingrich and President Bill Clinton magically put their differences aside and worked on the bill like two brothers who had been in business together for fifty years. The only time this happens in Washington is when the super elite donor class settles the score by saying we will equally fund both parties campaigns. Senate supporters included thirty-four Republicans and twenty-seven Democrats. In a big ceremony on December 8, 1993, during which Clinton essentially stated "NAFTA means jobs," he signed NAFTA into law.[6] That signature was three decades in the making; here's how NAFTA unfolded:

In the last mid-century, tariffs were having a negative impact on North America's auto industry, with the US shipping parts to Canada for them to assemble, rather than just shipping finished models. The cars that Canada built from American components carried the same brand names as in the US, but were built with slight modifications to differentiate theirs from ours. It was an expensive half-measure for all, and in 1965, President Lyndon Johnson and Prime Minister Lester Pearson signed the Canada-United States Automotive Products Agreement (APTA).

It removed the tariffs between Canada and the US to allow for a more seamless and integrated auto pipeline between the two countries for the big three car manufacturers—Ford, GM, and Chrysler (Volvo would later come onboard).

The agreement was largely considered a positive move, succeeding in both the lowering of prices and an increase of good-paying, new, blue-collar jobs in Canada, while streamlining the development and manufacturing sectors in the US auto industry. It got the elites thinking of linking more and having a global competition for wages.

Throughout the 1980s, while the impacts of the PATCO strike and recessions were being felt in America, Canada approached the US proposing a new bilateral venture. The Canada-United States Free Trade Agreement (CUSFTA) would eliminate even more barriers in the movement of services and goods, and liberalize investment opportunities between the two countries as well. The agreement would allow Canadians to travel to the US and buy goods tax-free, while providing Americans increased access to Canada's energy and cultural industries. In short, America would have cheaper access to commodities that aided in the manufacturing of goods that Canadians would be able to purchase at cheaper prices.

Canadians, fearing the potential impact on jobs and anxious about becoming America's "fifty-first state," resisted the agreement aggressively, though it ultimately passed in a referendum vote in 1988. The American people, on the other hand, paid little attention to the agreement, and CUSFTA breezed through Congress, with President Reagan signing it into law at the end of September that same year. Even blue-collar workers made little noise in the wake of continued auto production; still reeling from the ever-diminishing power of their unions, line workers were grateful for the employment and what benefits they could hold onto.

It turned out that Canadians were right to have been concerned. Subsequent years would see a rise in the Canadian dollar, which made their manufactured goods too expensive to produce and sell, and led to job losses in that sector. It was a lose-lose proposition because a recession that followed did little to help American industries.

Unbelievably, despite the damage, by the time Reagan's Vice President, George H.W. Bush, was in the White House, talks were already underway to expand the North American trade agreement to include Mexico. Assisted by the Advisory Committee for Trade Policy and Negotiations—which helped sell NAFTA to Congress—Bush asserted that by eliminating barriers between the three nations and by codifying agreements on agricultural, textile, and auto trade, as well as everything from mobility of workers to environmental policies and beyond, US corporations could relocate manufacturing production out of the country and sell products back to the US to everyone's benefit.[7] Bush signed the agreement in 1992—all that was needed was NAFTA's Congressional ratification. One might have thought that never would have happened because Bush lost the election to the Democrat Bill Clinton. Also, American labor workers woke up and weren't sold on the idea of shipping blue-collar jobs to Mexico. Organized labor retaliated and petitioned their elected officials to fight NAFTA, even as the giant retailer Walmart began opening stores in Mexico, claiming that the demand for American products couldn't be higher in the underserved market. Other companies like GE also began to move their businesses south of the border. By the summer of 1992, everything from clothes to processed food, to the more than a quarter-million cars and trucks sold in the US annually was being manufactured in Mexico.[8] And the bill hadn't even been ratified yet.

America had soured on President ("no new taxes") Bush by Election Day 1992, and Ross Perot's infomercials, while compelling, couldn't compare to the charismatic presence and persuasive message of Bill Clinton. He had risen from a fatherless childhood in the segregated South to become the governor of Arkansas, then, at forty-six, he would become the third-youngest president in history.

Clinton believed in more than "A Place Called Hope," and though he campaigned with less enthusiasm than Bush on NAFTA, he was far more supportive of the agreement's passage than Perot. In the end, it was Clinton's apparent concern for America's labor force and environmental protection standards that led to the caving of Congress sufficient to pass the measure.

It wasn't easy, and it turned out to be a fallacy. But unlike elite politicians (including the Yale-educated Bush and the Bilderberg donor classes with whom Clinton had consulted in 1991), Clinton was a better salesman when it came to NAFTA. To get his poll numbers up in the South, his campaign fed the media stories about Clinton owning an El Camino with carpet in the back. His humble background and craggy folksiness masked an Oxford pedigree and coziness with Wall Street, and downplayed the rarefied elite positions held by his wife, attorney

Hillary Rodham, who had only resigned her seat on the Board of Directors of Walmart to campaign alongside her husband. Governor Clinton had campaigned on the belief that his revised NAFTA—with its new protective regulatory standards and environmental codicils—would benefit everyone.

"Fair trade, not free trade" became the rallying cry, and the 1974 Trade Adjustment Assistance (TAA) Program for Dislocated Workers was expanded for those directly affected by NAFTA.[9]

The 1993 TAA plan would obligate the government to provide dislocated worker benefits for employees in manufacturing who might lose their jobs to Canada or Mexico, as well as help them to find a new job in their field.[10] It also offered reimbursement for relocating, and even career counseling with up to two years assistance in new job training—with an extra year of unemployment benefits included—in any job-related educational program in a field where they could expect to find work. The intentions of these measures might have been good, but the outcomes were bad because they did not fit the culture of a community where people want to be left alone. Had a career counselor asked my friend Eugene Kicklighter, "What would you like to do in a career?," the answer would have been,

"Work."

"Well, what kind of work?"

"It don't matter, just work."

A year after winning the election, Clinton suddenly switched and became a big proponent that NAFTA would "create 200,000 new high-paying jobs in the next two years," telling Americans not to fear the painful technological advances a new global economy required.[11] American workers, Clinton said, could "out-compete and out-perform anyone, anywhere." But he didn't say, "you are going to be competing against people making $2 an hour." And, you can mark this down: American businesses are very good at finding the lowest cost of production.

Clinton's pledge, combined with aggressive lobbying by retailers and manufacturers, would lead to the ratifying of NAFTA by comfortable margins in both houses by the end of his first year in office—though the support came predominantly from southern districts and not the Rust Belt.

It had taken three American presidents, but NAFTA finally went into effect on January 1, 1994. Immediately, more than half of Mexican exports and a third of US exports saw their tariffs lifted, resulting in a trade deficit that would grow by 576%.[12] It would end up costing the American people—particularly the rural and industrial workers—nearly one million jobs. Plus, the wage floor completely fell out on the jobs that didn't leave town, due to a lack of wage competition.

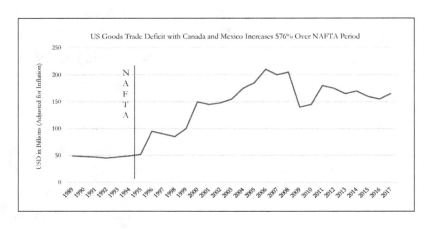

US Goods Trade Deficit with Canada and Mexico Increases 576% Over NAFTA Period

IN THE ECONOMIC policy institute's excellent 2013 overview, "NAFTA's Impact on US Workers," Founding President and Distinguished Fellow Jeff Faux wrote of the principal ways in which the trade agreement devastated the working poor, benefitted elites, and further decimated the working class over the span of ten short years:

> First, it caused the loss of some 700,000 jobs as production moved to Mexico. ... To be sure, there were some job gains along the border in service and retail sectors resulting from increased trucking activity, but these gains are small in relation to the losses, and are in lower paying occupations. The vast majority of workers who lost jobs from NAFTA suffered a permanent loss of income.[13] ...

In Waycross—and in other areas where Renegades had been barely hanging on—the effects were nothing short of catastrophic. The number of unemployed and underemployed grew at a rate the government's TAA program couldn't keep up with.[14] Moreover, the TAA qualifying criteria, even adjusted for NAFTA, failed to include many categories of workers who were displaced; fewer laid-off workers qualified, or had done the work to qualify, for government assistance. In addition, about one-third of jobs lost weren't directly as a result of NAFTA per se, but in nonmanufacturing, service areas of the economy; when factories closed, it crushed the obligation chain in the entire area. For example, when someone tells the State Farm agent, "I can't pay you," then the State Farm agent can't pay someone else because they don't have the money. Perot should have had, in his charts, two studies: obligation chain and wage economics destruction. And then viewers would have been able to see that NAFTA killed much more than jobs; it killed communities.

In 2016, the year Donald Trump was making his Make America Great Again (MAGA) pledge, the average displaced manufacturing worker, lucky enough to find another job, had seen their $40,000 annual salary decreased by almost $8,000 in forty years. In short, the 2.8M Renegade who had lost their jobs were scraping by with multiple, lower-income jobs; and those still on a line somewhere had seen their income drop a further 20%. EPI's Faux also wrote:

> As soon as NAFTA became law, corporate managers began telling their workers that their companies intended to move to Mexico unless the workers lowered the cost of their labor. In the midst of collective bargaining negotiations with unions, some companies would even start loading machinery into trucks that they said were bound for Mexico. The same threats were used to fight union organizing efforts. The message was: 'If you vote in a union, we will move south of the border.'

And workers thought the PATCO fallout was bad. It didn't matter how successful your company was; in fact, sometimes, a factory's very stability played the largest factor in causing employment insecurity. By the end of the last century, 68%

of manufacturing, distribution, and wholesale/distribution employers had threatened their labor force against union activity, and into lower wages and working conditions. Finally, Faux wrote:

> *Third, the destructive effect of NAFTA on the Mexican agricultural and small business sectors dislocated several million Mexican workers and their families, and was a major cause in the dramatic increase in undocumented workers flowing into the US labor market. This put further downward pressure on US wages, especially in the already lower paying market for less skilled labor.[15]...*

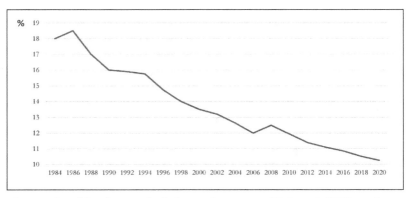

A reminder of the chart we looked at early on, page 37. Since PATCO, we have seen about an 80% decline in unionization.

One of the benefits of NAFTA for the US—and especially farmers—was that it allowed government-subsidized agricultural products, particularly corn, to flow into Mexico. Local farmers south of the border, however, couldn't compete without moving to cheaper land (which increased deforestation) and using more fertilizers and chemicals. By decade's end, some

900,000 farming jobs in Mexico would be lost to NAFTA.[16] And while American workers saw their jobs vanish, employment exploded for Mexicans willing to work for American companies in assembly shops near the border. These *maquiladora* factories doubled in number as a result of NAFTA, and by 1994, 58% of Mexican exports derived from this highly exploited labor force, who worked for a fraction of an American worker's comparable wages.[17] By 2006, some 1.2 million Mexicans were toiling in these sweatshops.[18] I think global trade is good, and it is naïve to think we could have signed agreements demanding other countries meet, dollar-for-dollar, our standard of living. But we could have asked for a *pro rata* trade deal, where Mexico would have had to raise their labor wages to the equivalent of ours. For example, our $20-per-hour wage could convert to $5 per hour in Mexico, allowing workers to at least compete in a range of fairness, although heavily tilted against American workers. We should have demanded the same environmental standards on both sides, since we all live on the same planet. However, NAFTA was never about fairness in trade and competition; it was about redistribution of wealth to Wall Street.

Between the fertilizers and the waste from the border factories, pollution in Mexico increased exponentially. Between the loss of farms and slave wages at the border, Mexicans increasingly crossed into the US looking for work, leading to an immigration surge—and more. The free movement of goods between America and Mexico meant that *all* goods went into play—including the drug trade, which would impact those most hurt by NAFTA, in abundance.

Let me be the first to say, Perot was right about the giant

sucking sound. Clinton and the Congress were wrong on NAFTA. But the latter two had to fund their campaigns from the elite donor class. From 1994 onwards, working, living, and environmental standards were being decimated across rural and industrial North America as well as in Mexico. All as a result of NAFTA. I'm glad to see others came around, including the guy who led Congress, Newt Gingrich:

> *NAFTA was the final result of a process that began with Ronald Reagan in 1979. It had 14 years of effort and was central to North American progress. We are now in a different era. 23 years after that vote it is clear that a lot of our trade efforts are destructive. When the director of national intelligence staff reports that China stole $360 billion in intellectual property last year, twice our total sales to China, there is something profoundly wrong.[19]*

Despite the misery NAFTA inflicted on so many, the trade agreement boosted economic growth by as much as 0.5% a year, with agricultural and automotive sectors among those that benefitted most. Business was fine for everyone who was buying and everyone who was selling—all at the expense of those doing the actual *making* and those who weren't making anything anymore.

ACCORDING TO THE economic policy institute's study on the effects of NAFTA, one factor was ultimately the most important, and had the most far-reaching impact, as the EPI's Faux wrote:

> NAFTA was the template for rules of the emerging global economy, in which the benefits would flow to capital and the costs to labor. The US governing class—in alliance with the financial elites of its trading partners—applied NAFTA's principles to the World Trade Organization, to the policies of the World Bank and IMF, and to the deal under which employers of China's huge supply of low-wage workers were allowed access to US markets in exchange for allowing American multinational corporations the right to invest there.[20]

For Wall Street, the NAFTA '90s were good times indeed. Then the Dow went from 3,754.09 points on December 31, 1993 to 11,497.12 points on December 31, 1999.[21] On January 1, 1995—exactly one year after NAFTA went into effect—the United States became one of 123 countries to sign on to the World Trade Organization, a new international trade agreement replacing the antiquated General Agreement on Tariffs and Trades (GATT) that had been signed in 1947 to eliminate barriers to multinational trade.[22] Within five years, China entered into the agreement, and America's focus shifted to new business opportunities with an even cheaper labor force than Mexico's. The race to the bottom was on, and led to increased suffering for American, Mexican, and now Chinese laborers—all to the profit of Wall Street elites, the donor and governing classes, and the Bilderberg elites, who were all seeing their dream of a seamless global economy—run by themselves—coming to fruition (see Chapter 9). International monetary policy was permanently upended, with profits rewarding capital and losses falling on labor at an increasingly global scale—and the wealth accumulation went nuclear for the richest, whose fortunes have tripled on average in the last quarter century.

In 1992, an aspirant to the *Forbes* 400 would need at least $373.7 million in personal wealth; today, that number is $2.1 billion. There are currently 204 billionaires in the United States who fail to qualify for the list. Not all, but most of those billionaires were made on the backs of the 2.8M Renegade who showed up and voted for Trump.

Trump still had the green light from the 2.8M Renegade. Why? He still acts like he cares with some basic fairness in trade with China and trade agreements overall. Far worse than Trump's tactics on tax cuts are Clinton and Obama signing trade agreements with no labor and environmental standards, and totally walking away from the core principle of the Democratic Party: moving people from working class to middle class.

Despite all the rhetoric, the central goal of NAFTA was not expanding trade between the three nations. It never was. NAFTA will always be remembered as a boon to globally rigged capitalism that broke America and broke the spirit of the 2.8M Renegade.

Until November 2016.

But before that, NAFTA had another gift for the rural poor. In seemingly no time at all, the drug wars, legal and illegal, set about feasting on the bodies and souls of Americans from all walks of life, none more so than the desperately impoverished and disenfranchised Renegade population.

CHAPTER 7

Mile Marker 3

Misery Loves Company—The Opioid Addiction Crisis

~

"...were it left to me to decide whether we should have a government without newspapers or newspapers without a government, I should not hesitate a moment to prefer the latter."
~ *Thomas Jefferson*

SCREWED AGAIN. By 2000, six years after NAFTA's destruction, small towns like Waycross had gone from being vibrant communities full of mom-and-pop stores to trailer parks, Walmarts, and people just getting by. The youngest of the 2.8M Renegades were fifty years old, often with kids and grandkids, and it was *misery loves company.* Denial and malaise had set in.

It was in this moment that the super-elite-owned pharmaceutical industry and the government in charge of drug regulation, together, found a way to take over the rural landscape with a one-two addiction punch. They provided chemical brain candy in the form of pseudoephedrine and opioids to cope with the pains of living in squalor conditions. The brain candy was the final step in severing a portion of the American population from the rest of society for good, leaving them for dead.

The Walking Dead was a reality ten years before it became a hit TV show. When I visited my high school in 2006, which had now become Waycross High (they desegregated the schools in 1988, twenty years after the Civil Rights Bill was signed), the high school principal told me she was not so much worried about the students being on drugs, it was the parents who were on drugs and that the schools had to take care of the children. In 2020, *The New York Times* reported on a solution that health officials in rural Carter County, Tennessee, were employing. It was a new strategy in the battle to stem the damage to their community by opioid abuse: teaching children—as young as age six—to administer the nasal spray Narcan to a parent in danger of overdosing on an opioid.[1]

Nolan Loveday, age ten, with a Narcan dose during training in administering Narcan to parents in the event of an overdose. Photo credit to: Mike Belleme.

U.S. County Prescribing Rates, 2018

< U.S. County Prescribing Rates, 2017   U.S. Prescribing Rate Maps

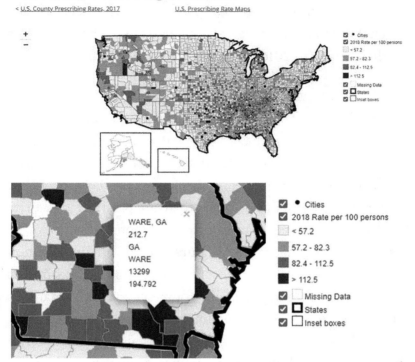

See above chart outlining the rates of opioid prescription within the United States—you can see the collection of "hot spots" in the smaller cities, where prescription is at an all-time high. I have zoomed in on the small town of Ware, Georgia to show the damage in these small towns. Data pulled from CDC.[2]

In 2014, across Tennessee—a state of 6.5 million people—8.1 million painkiller prescriptions were written.[3] So many of the 2.8M Renegades who voted for Trump had seen their kids and grandkids hooked on drugs and living in a war-zone-like environment their whole lives. But they can remember a time before PATCO, before NAFTA, before opioids, when they had a strong community and strong lives. They remember a time when rules and discipline were the highest priority in a country home. A shirttail hanging out was a near capital offense. You came to dinner with your hair combed, another reverie. That all changed to what is today a living nightmare. That's what was in their minds in 2016 when they voted for Trump.

THE BETRAYAL WAS more than a political theory, it was the road to addiction. Hopelessness is the super-spreader of addiction, and that includes alcohol. Boom or bust, alcohol has long been a feature of the addiction landscape in America, in all walks of life. When there are no jobs, people have more time at home, so more alcohol. When there are plenty of jobs, there is plenty of money so more alcohol to go around, but knocking back a few during working hours was out of the question by a blue-collar labor force of millworkers and machinists who worked in dangerous environments around hazardous chemicals capable of causing injury and death, even in sober hands. When there were jobs, there was also money to buy a bass boat to go fishing and a shotgun to go hunting—neither of which can be safely done under the influence of alcohol.

With the destruction caused by NAFTA, Big Pharma knew it had a new hoard of potential customers in these communities that were devastated; it was in the now-hopeless lives of people living in the country of cornstalks, coon hunts, and generations of clean living that Big Pharma saw an easy target.

Chemical stimulants have been around since the end of the 19th century in America. Everyone from the medical community to the army has utilized man-made derivatives of the ephedra plant, which had been a component of Chinese medicine for over 5,000 years. In a crystallized form, "amphetamines" were suitable for injecting, inhaling, and snorting, to treat everything from hyperactivity to obesity. Benzedrine, the first pharmaceutically marketed amphetamine, was introduced in 1959 and marketed as an aid in weight loss. "Speed" provided soldiers in Vietnam with the ability to stay awake and be energized—but left them with severe addictions that they brought home. At this point, the road to meth was being built.[4] The FDA finally intervened to stem rampant abuse when, citing heart risks and psychosis, the Controlled Substance Act of 1970s classified amphetamines as a Schedule II drug, a drug with a high potential for abuse.

After that, meth production went underground where it was manufactured primarily by motorcycle and street gangs. It was also easy to make if you knew how—it could be "cooked" with any of a number of household products, so long as it was combined with a component found in amphetamines which, while then more regulated, was still available.

Then, in 1980, that key chemical found in amphetamines— Phenyl-2-propanone—also came under federal regulation.[5] Rather than curb meth production, the cooks discovered that cold remedy ingredients—ephedrine and pseudoephedrine— not only worked as substitutes but had double the potency of the old meth.

Pure ephedrine powder wasn't available in America, but while news outlets, politicians, and even Hollywood focused on the cocaine craze and heroin abuses of the 1980s and 1990s, the meth epidemic got very little attention, even as drug traffickers based in Mexico took over the motorcycle gangs to produce higher quality and more potent meth, and more and more addicts turned to cooking their own.[6]

Legislation was proposed in 1986 that would have monitored the sales and import records of the companies producing ephedrine and pseudoephedrine along with the cold medicines, diet pills, and other products derived from them, but the pharmaceutical industry threw a ton of money and might into lobbying against the legislation.[7] In the end, the monitoring of purchases and sales of ephedrine and pseudoephedrine excluded manufacturers of pills, like Sudafed and Claritin-D, which contained the chemicals. By 2013, Big Pharma was pulling a $605 million profit from pseudoephedrine-based drugs annually.[8]

Lawmakers in twenty-five states had attempted to make pseudoephedrine a prescription drug, succeeding only in Mississippi and Oregon. Even half-measures like cumbersome packaging for cold and allergy meds were continually defeated by a well-compensated Congress. Instead, lawmakers focused their attention on punitive action directed toward those who made and were addicted to the byproduct of the drug they refused to regulate; people who were predominantly rural, poor, and at the end of their ropes—courtesy of union-busting and NAFTA. Between 1994—the year NAFTA was signed into law—and 2004, methamphetamine use rose from just under 2% of America's adult population to approximately 5%.[9] By 2008, approximately thirteen million people over age twelve would have used meth at least once.[10] Between 2015 and 2018, the Centers for Disease Control and Prevention (CDC) found that more than half (53%) of the 1.6 million meth users were addicted to it, and noted that many of them also used other drugs and suffered from mental illness.[11]

THE METH MADE in trailer parks was extremely dangerous and addictive. Fortunately, making it on a kitchen stove could not scale for the drug trafficking runaway demands in those communities. In came big pharmaceuticals to fill the demand with such a business passion that you could almost call them "Opioids, Inc."

Opioids also have a long history in America, dating back to the Civil War when medications, derived from the opium poppy, such as morphine, codeine, and heroin, were administered to soldiers and later sold as medications and cure-alls.[12] Later, synthetic derivatives like fentanyl (the "pain-patch," introduced in 1990) tended to be more potent.[13] By the mid-20th century, as the addictive qualities of opioids became more well known, their use was severely curtailed by the medical and dental establishments, reserved for post-surgical and end-of-life patients, or for those recovering from severe trauma and acute pain.

In the 1990s, the pharmaceutical industry had begun to scale operations for large demands and heavily market promotions of opioids as a safe treatment for chronic non-cancer pain. This was due almost entirely to the launch of OxyContin in December 1995. It was an oxycodone pill with a special coating, which its manufacturer, Purdue Pharma, proclaimed resulted in a time-release dosage that would prevent the seductive *rush* that led to addiction. But the rush could still be experienced by simply crushing or even cutting the oil to render the coating ineffective, and that twelve-hour window didn't last for many of its patients, leading to painful and anxiety-filled withdrawal and overuse, and dangerously increased dosage prescriptions to perpetuate the "twelve-hour" efficacy myth.[14]

Over the next five years, Purdue Pharma combed databases for physicians with high opioid prescription rates and presumably higher numbers of chronic pain patients.[15] Sales reps approached these physicians with incentives, including free, limited-time prescriptions—a program that culminated in over 34,000 redemptions for patients and a total of $40 million in incentive bonuses for sales reps in a single year. Sales reps for Perdue Pharma, and other opioid manufacturers, like Johnson & Johnson and Allergan, were being propelled into rarefied elite status, one prescription at a time.

It was OxyContin, however, that opened the opioid floodgates, aggressively targeting America's rural poor, especially Appalachia, from the start—infusing states like West Virginia and Kentucky with millions of pills, first through prescription and then through black market doctors, pharmacies, street dealers—and the US government. [16, 17]

In a special broadcast on the opioid crisis televised on *60 Minutes*, it was revealed by drug manufacturer Ed Thompson that, in 2001, the Food and Drug Administration itself had a major role in the opioid crisis.[18] According to Thompson, the FDA—under pressure by Big Pharma—approved OxyContin for use for chronic and common ailments such as arthritis and back pain. Without any science to back its decision, in 2001, the FDA changed OxyContin from an end-of-life drug into a lifestyle drug.

Seven years later, in 2008, some 51,000 kids between ages twelve and seventeen were reported to use pain relievers non-medically—part of the 360,000 Georgians abusing drugs at the time: nearly 5% of the population. In April that same year, a group of third-graders at Center Elementary in Waycross brought handcuffs, tape, and a steak knife to school, planning to use them against their teacher.[19] The kids were nine years old. By April of 2009, the unemployment rate in Georgia was 9.3%, compared to 8.9% nationally.[20] In Ware County, unemployment was at 13.3% by 2009.[21]

By 2018, four years after the Affordable Care Act expanded in 2014, 97.5 million costing as little as $1 for as many as 240 pills.

The party line was that rural populations were, on average, older than urban ones, who presumably needed more pain management. Blue-collar labor forces also experienced more body strain and work injuries—when they had worked—and OxyContin and Vicodin would help alleviate suffering there. Renegade Country, drug manufacturers concluded, was a perfect dumping ground for opioids.

"Dumping ground" isn't hyperbole. A pharmacy in Kermit, West Virginia (population 400), received over three million prescription opioids in the space of ten months. Between 2006 and 2016, nearly twenty-one million hydrocodone and oxycodone pills were dispensed from two pharmacies in Williamson alone.[22, 23] This averaged out to 6,500 pills per resident of this coal-mining town on the West Virginia/Kentucky border. From Los Angeles to Georgia, drug seekers began getting multiple prescriptions from as many as five doctors and purchasing drugs off the street; young people were stealing from their parents' supplies when they ran out of pills prescribed by their doctors and caregivers. The pull of addiction was that strong. When all else failed, opioid addicts increasingly began turning to cheaper and more effective alternatives—heroin, and eventually, the highly lethal drug fentanyl.[24]

By 2014, nearly half a million Americans had died from drug overdoses, with more cases reported that year than in any previous year on record.[25] In that year, 61% of drug deaths were due to opioids, with more people dying from overdoses than car crashes. Heroin deaths had tripled over four years; states with significant increases in drug deaths that year included Virginia, Alabama, Ohio, Pennsylvania, Maine, New Hampshire, Maryland—and Georgia.

It also didn't help that in President Obama's last year in office, he signed the Ensuring Patient Access and Effective Drug Enforcement Act, essentially handcuffing the Drug Enforcement Administration (DEA). The 2016 Act amended the Controlled Substances Act to redefine the DEA's "authority to register manufacturers, distributors, and dispensers of controlled substances."[26] Before the 2016 Act, the DEA was able to immediately suspend a registration to prevent "imminent danger to the public health and safety." But the 2016 Act expanded the "imminent danger" definition, and the elements for the DEA, to show cause before it could deny, revoke, or suspend a registration. The 2016 Act states that "An order to show cause must specifically state the legal basis for the action and notify the registrant of the opportunity to submit a corrective action plan," and that the FDA, the CDC—including the DEA—must report to Congress a laundry list of justifications for its actions.

According to a 2017 article in *The Washington Post*, the 2016 Act was an alliance between some members of Congress and major drug makers to create a law that was friendlier to industry, but would ultimately undermine "efforts to staunch the flow of pain pills."[27] The 2016 Act was:

> ... *the crowning achievement of a multifaceted campaign by the drug industry to weaken aggressive DEA enforcement efforts against drug distribution companies that were supplying corrupt doctors and pharmacists who peddled narcotics to the black market. The industry worked behind the scenes with lobbyists and key members of Congress, pouring more than a million dollars into their election campaigns.*
>
> *The chief advocate of the law that hobbled the DEA was Rep. Tom Marino, a Pennsylvania Republican who is now President Donald Trump's nominee to become the nation's next drug czar. Marino spent years trying to move the law through Congress. It passed after Sen. Orrin Hatch, R-Utah, negotiated a final version with the DEA.*
>
> *... It sailed through Congress without debate and was passed by unanimous consent, a parliamentary procedure reserved for bills considered to be noncontroversial.*

... A senior DEA official said the agency fought the bill for years in the face of growing pressure from key members of Congress and industry lobbyists. But the DEA lost the battle and eventually was forced to accept a deal it did not want.

...Marino declined repeated requests for comment. Marino's staff called the Capitol Police when The Post and 60 Minutes tried to interview the congressman at his office. ... In the past, the congressman has said the DEA was too aggressive and needed to work more collaboratively with drug companies.

The law gained momentum in 2015, when the Justice Department named a new DEA chief— Rosenberg—who said he wanted to mend the rift between the agency and the drug industry.

"Rosenberg wanted to paint a new face on the DEA for the Hill," said Regina LaBelle, the chief of staff for the White House's Officer of National Drug Control Policy at the time. "He wanted to show them the softer side of the DEA, and he wanted to work with industry."[28]

BY 2015, PURDUE PHARMA reported sales topping $35 billion, propelling the company's owners, the Sackler family, onto that year's Forbes list of America's richest families.[29] Their (conservative) net worth at the time: $14 billion, placing them at number sixteen. Elites celebrated the philanthropy of the family, whose name graced wings of museums from the

Metropolitan Museum of Art to the Louvre, and who endowed universities including Oxford, Harvard, Columbia, NYU, and the University of Edinburgh.

There had been setbacks along the way for the Sacklers and OxyContin—but they hadn't lasted long. In 2007, Purdue Pharma had pled guilty to federal charges of misleading doctors, regulators, and patients about the risks of their drug, paying $600 million in fines and penalties for, among other issues, pushing the sales of their higher-dose pills over cheaper lower doses.[30] Shortly after, Purdue enlisted the management consulting firm of McKinsey & Company who, for five years, helped strategize against subsequent diminishing profits. Their suggestions included focusing on the most prolific opioid prescribers, as well as pushing back against government efforts to stop illegal opioid prescribing.

Still, in the wake of what was now regarded as an "opioid epidemic" in the mainstream news, Purdue Pharma was looking for ways to increase profits. In September 2014, the company decided to enter into a new and thriving industry— medication for the very addiction it had created.[31] With OxyContin sales declining, Purdue Pharma's confidential in-house study, code-named "Project Tango," concluded that the company would become an "end-to-end pain provider," and turned its focus to the overdose-reversing drugs Suboxone and Narcan.[32] As late as 2018, Dr. Richard Sackler, son of Purdue Pharma's founder Raymond, received a patent for a drug to treat addiction, according to a civil complaint filed by the state of Massachusetts against Purdue Pharma, company directors, executives, and eight members of the

Sackler Family.[33] As of fall 2019, forty-eight states and two thousand local governments had taken legal action against the Sacklers and their company, by which time the State of New York charged the Sackler family with draining more than $4 billion from Purdue Pharma over a dozen years amid mounting worries of legal threats.[34] The Sacklers succeeded in sequestering their wealth in a tangle of trusts and shell companies, often in offshore tax havens—including the transfer of $1 billion in wire transfers through Swiss and their hidden accounts. At that point, their wealth all but untouchable, Purdue Pharma filed for bankruptcy. By November, a federal bankruptcy judge extended protection, halting scores of lawsuits against the Sacklers and Purdue Pharma until April 2020.[35]

OPIOID INC. IS a demonstration of the super elites doing their best work. Before the three milestones, addiction where I come from was probably about the same as the rest of the country. But since PATCO, NAFTA, and Opioid Inc., it is a drug-infested wasteland. And it's important to remember that the three milestones were premeditated, which Merriam-Webster defines as "(of an action, especially a crime) thought out or planned beforehand."[36] They were premeditated to cause destruction on a vulnerable, non-participating society so that the super elites could make a lot of money. If the super elites had tried to do this to a vibrant community that participated, they would be voted out. And that went on for forty-five years, until the 2.8M Renegade saw a glimmer of hope and a reverie in Donald Trump.

CHAPTER 8

~o———o~

Finger Lickin' Bad—
Southern Fare to Fast Food

~

EARLIER, I GAVE you an insider's look at what life used to be like for the 2.8M Renegade (see Chapter 4), and that included a desire for an unchanging world—again, change is not a part of their makeup, and they would be happiest in a world that always stays the same.

But their world did change post PATCO, NAFTA, and Opioids Inc.

One of the biggest changes I've seen in the country lifestyle is the diet; they adapted to a diet of fast food fare. From right after the Revolutionary War until the 1970s, plain Southern fare was the heart of the country Renegade diet—rice and peas, gravy, sliced tomatoes, turnip greens, cornbread, butter beans, and bacon or hamburger steak.

For today's 2.8M Renegade, those meals are long gone. Even fast food is being replaced by the frozen food case of pizzas and burritos at the dollar-brand retail chains. A long tradition of not wanting to be bothered about public policy or civic affairs set the stage for all the dollar-brand stores, where minimum wage paychecks can afford "something to eat" on almost a day-by-day basis.[1] The reason dollar-brand stores are so profitable is that the buyer ultimately ends up paying more for less, but it's all they can do to scrape together enough money to buy either something to eat that day or bathroom soap to bathe that night. The whole merchandising strategy is to provide less in quantity at higher prices per unit.

Even where a few of the grocery stores have stayed, they jack up their prices as compared to a grocery store in the city where jobs are more plentiful and paychecks are much larger. Here are findings reported in the *Atlanta Journal-Constitution* of items in a rural Georgia Piggly Wiggly versus a Kroger in Metro Atlanta.

	Piggly Wiggly in Rural Georgia	Metro Kroger in Atlanta	Comparison
Iceberg lettuce	$2.99	$1.49	100% higher
American cheese	$4.99	$3.39	33% higher
Spaghetti	$1.79	$1.00	44% higher
Green beans	$1.19	$0.65	33% higher

Look at how much more expensive basic food is in the smaller, lower income rural areas compared to metropolitan stores in the state of Georgia. Data pulled from Atlanta Journal-Constitution.[2]

According to a review by *The Atlanta Journal-Constitution*, rural Georgians are more likely to need the help of food stamps to pay for their groceries, but that public help doesn't stretch as far as it does in places such as Atlanta because of higher food prices in small-town stores, creating, for rural residents, a double whammy: fewer opportunities to earn a living combined with higher food prices to survive.[3]

Number of SNAP Recipients		
County	Population	Percentage of SNAP recipients
Dawson	2,928	34%
Blakely	2,842	27.7%
Fort Gaines	775	26.8%
Georgetown	592	26%
Cordele	5,822	25.8%
Colquitt	1,450	25.5%
Donalsonville	2,084	25.1%
Claxton	2,633	24.8%
Cuthbert	1,694	24.8%
Fitzgerald	4,121	24.5%

A striking percentage of the population in rural Georgia counties are on food stamps. All of the above are known as "farming communities." But here's a big secret—farms are long gone; they're not even a minimum factor in these communities anymore.[4]

NAFTA made food insecurity no longer just a pervasive problem faced by foreign countries; it exists all over what might be called the "farmland." In Terrell County, Georgia, 3,300 out of a population of 8,600 people, making up more than 38% of all residents, receive food stamps.[5] And it is pervasive: twenty-five zip codes in the US with the highest rates of people receiving food stamps are all in rural Georgia. You have to understand:

NAFTA wiped out everything in Georgia but metro Atlanta, which, by the way, had the twenty-five zip codes with the lowest food stamps disbursements and lower grocery prices on fresher products. Poor rural Georgians pay more for tomatoes, cheese, and other foods because there is little competition for their business. Get out of your head the idea that the region is full of farmers; there are actually few farms remaining in rural Georgia, and those that are left grow one bounty crop like cotton or corn. You can drive one hundred miles and more before you see anything close to a Farmer's Market.

Today, rural America reminds me of my trip to Cuba and has two of the same problems: stuck in time and just sucks for having no money. Keith Orejel, a professor who studies rural communities, told Yahoo Finance that the "plight of rural America was much more structural." And that, "When one gets down to brass tacks, at the end of day, rural areas never recovered from the Great Recession."[6] Great Recession? Are you kidding me? The Great Depression started in 1994 for these people, and things have been going downhill ever since.

Can you understand the 2.8M Renegade rationale: You took my job, you made me poor, and then you gave me higher food prices to survive. And you made money off the deal by investing in chains with predatory profits, that sell me that higher-priced, worse food.

Then, along comes a candidate who makes no bones about some of his favorite foods being fast food from McDonald's and KFC—do you see a parallel?[7]

WITH POOR DIETS comes poor health. The CDC says the highest rates of type 2 diabetes in the US are in a "diabetes belt," a 644-county span across southern states. With Medicare and Medicaid funding, there is a lot of money to be made in the belt because there is a density of disease paid for by Medicare in the population. Wall Street rolled out the money for diabetes medical devices, disposable needles, and software for insulin distribution in hospitals and homes. The elites have made more money off people they made poor than they have each other, since the elites are, by design, quite stingy among "friends."

But poor diets have also led to increases in obesity, high blood pressure, and a list of you-name-it ailments. Yet even as nutrition-related illnesses and deaths have increased exponentially over the last quarter century, access to hospitals and adequate health has diminished drastically in rural America, with 106 rural hospitals shutting down since 2011.[8, 9] And with a deficit of over four thousand doctors in rural areas, the question of Medicaid and Medicare is moot for the uninsured/underinsured 2.8M Renegade.[10] Without access to caregivers, the 2.8M Renegade is often forced to travel hundreds of miles and camp out to receive treatment in emergency makeshift clinics, staffed by volunteer doctors—and dentists.[11] So, now the 2.8M Renegade rationale is this: You took my job, you charged me higher food prices, you made me fat, and then you made money off me being fat and sick—because you've got this big fat wallet called "Uncle Sam."

A mouthful of unhealthy teeth is another 2.8M Renegade attribute. Today, 98% of the people in the Appalachian region of the US experience tooth decay by age forty-four, so is it any wonder the term "Mountain Dew Mouth" has come to refer to more than just the tooth decay that accompanies the frequent consumption of soft drinks?[12] I was fortunate to come from a family that enjoyed a rarer level of dental care than many people enjoy, whether in the South or other areas of the US. Daddy had Golden Cadillac benefits through his railroad job, and Mary worked at a dentist's office. Daddy married Mary when I was age five. I remember seeing Dad flossing in the mirror often, and he and Mary often told us, "You got to have good teeth to get a good job." Any recovery solution for a true Renegade must include a good job with medical *and* dental coverage.

That coverage must also take care of mental health. Help for physical ailments in rural areas is hard enough to come by, but help for mental health is not even on the radar. Much as my brother Kenny thrived growing up on a farm, the repetitive tasks he was assigned were the only therapy for his behavioral challenges, which we would now diagnose as a solid case of ADHD. Kenny never received treatment, as his lack of ability to concentrate and subsequent outbursts at school were regarded as a discipline problem. Our lives began to change after Daddy married Mary and she began to build a wall between us and him. After our brother Matt was born, Mary gained full leverage over Daddy, and he turned away from the rest of us kids emotionally. With a withdrawn father and disapproving stepmom who found plenty of reasons to keep him in trouble, Kenny turned to alcohol and drug addiction at the earliest opportunity. My sister Beth appeared to have the best mental health of us all. She was focused, disciplined, listened when my dad spoke, and, encouraged by our Grandmama, tried to have a relationship with Mary. But as with all of us, Mary just let her down and put her down, and had Beth believing as we all did that she would be put out of the house (and in Mary's mind, out of Waycross). Like Kenny, I struggled with ADHD, which I sought treatment for later in life. My main addiction, however, was and remains workaholism, which can be as destructive as any chemical addiction.

WHEN IT COMES to work, the 2.8M Renegade has historically not had careers—they've had *jobs*—jobs that predominantly involved labor, both skilled and otherwise. While I was growing up in Georgia, a high school education was pretty much required to work at a plant, operate machinery, or learn a trade, so most 2.8M Renegades strove for that, or at least a GED. When railroad and factory jobs were available, pre-NAFTA, everyone I knew in Waycross was dead set on getting a high school diploma to get one of those jobs. It was rare for anyone not to graduate. The loss of factory jobs changed all that. When those jobs left town, in the eyes of youth in Waycross, there was no longer a need to finish high school. It doesn't take much learning to work at Burger King or Dollar General, so when the job opportunities vanished, the desire for advancement began to increasingly be replaced with the need to survive. Today, any available job is accepted as an opportunity.

But the elites even see opportunity in those who still have hope for a future. President Obama himself backed off holding private schools accountable for graduation rates if they received federal funds. So while the 2.8M Renegade can pursue a college degree, they often pursue for-profit college TV degrees, which are financed by the federal government. These degrees often end up straddling the student with so much debt that they can't afford to live. A study by WalletHub found that more than 83% of cities with the worst student-to-debt ratio were in the South, with student loans comprising from 68% to 85% of their income, or median debt of around $17,000–$21,000 on annual earnings of $21,000–$25,000.[13]

You would expect to see large amounts of student debt in the larger metropolitan cities but surprisingly, it's in rural areas and not big cities. And it creates a vicious cycle for the people in those smaller towns: they want to pay for an education, but are then plagued with such large debt that they are stuck in their small town, unable to afford going anywhere else.

NOW THAT I'VE painted a clearer picture of the subculture of the 2.8M Renegade, let's take a look at the subculture at the other end of the spectrum—the super elites.

CHAPTER 9

Rhinestone Elites
Become Super

~

DURING HIS CAMPAIGN, Trump initially relied heavily on the phrase "drain the swamp." But "drain the swamp" is a phrase used by both US political parties to describe how they intend to rid Washington DC of the real or perceived corruption. Closer to the truth is that the political "swamp" is actually a lot of opportunistic people working and living in a world called the US Capitol with a lot of money floating around, called the Federal Treasury. Result? They have made it legal to get rich in public service. Decent politicians like John McCain used to say, "Sure it [campaign contributions] has an influence on us and we need to fix it."

Nancy Pelosi told John Stewart on "The Daily Show" that she could raise 30 million with no opponent and the money had zero influence, at least that is what her mouth was saying, but her face and eyes were saying something else.[1] Washington DC is totally dark in money, buying outcomes from NAFTA to the FDA, to the belief in "too big to fail." All outcomes come from the same place—the elite donor class.

"Draining the swamp," therefore, became one group of opportunistic people swapping out for another group, with the elite donor class controlling the agenda both ways. Thereby, no one drained the swamp—they just refilled it with their people. By the way, technically, you cannot drain a swamp. Where I grew up in the Okefenokee Swamp, in 1891, a couple of swashbuckling timber entrepreneurs came up with a plan to drain large portions of the basin—a 438,000-acre, peat-filled wetland—so they could get man and machine to the virgin timber deep in its waters. They poured investor money into building the Suwanee Canal to unplug the swamp basin and drain it. What they did not know is that the swamp has an elegant hydraulic system that absorbs water like a sponge during floods, and then releases water during droughts. To the entrepreneurs and their investors' surprise, the man-made canal drain flipped the swamp switch and it filled to the brim; the water table in the swamp actually rose—just like the wealth from Trump's tax cut when he proclaimed to drain the swamp. The swamp said no. A political swamp cannot be drained when both ends of it are owned by the same super elite.

THE MODERN DAY political swamp dates back to 1954, when a core group of world leaders, media titans, academics, industrialists, and bankers from Europe and the United States gathered in the Netherlands at the Hotel de Bilderberg with the intention of not only avoiding future world wars, but also of fostering understanding and cooperation between nations on defense, economic, and political levels.

Since then, the Bilderberg Group, as it came to be known, has continued to hold an annual conference, hosted by revolving nations and attended by both a core group of members and specifically chosen guests. The meetings are private—the press is strictly forbidden—and the guest list is equally secret, although it's widely known that the Council on Foreign Relations, the International Monetary Fund, the European Union, and every entity from the World Bank to the International Monetary Fund are consistently represented.[2] Everyone from Henry Kissinger to Rupert Murdoch, from Barack Obama to Alan Greenspan, from George Soros to Donald Rumsfeld has attended the conference; 2019's guest list for the conference, held in Montreux, France, included Kissinger, Jared Kushner, Governor of the Bank of England Mark Carney, and Secretary of State Mike Pompeo.

According to the website, Bilderbergmeetings.org:

Since its inaugural Meeting in 1954, the annual Bilderberg Meeting has been a forum for informal discussions to foster dialogue between Europe and North America. Every year, approx. 130 political leaders and experts from industry, finance, labour, academia and the media are invited to take part in the Meeting. About two thirds of the participants come from Europe and the rest from North America; one third from politics and government and the rest from other fields. The Meeting is a forum for informal discussions about major issues. The Meetings are held under the Chatham House Rule, which states that participants are free to use the information received, but neither the identity nor the affiliation of the speaker(s) nor of any other participant may be revealed. Thanks to the private nature of the Meeting, the participants take part as individuals rather than in any official capacity, and hence are not bound by the conventions of their office or by pre-agreed positions. As such, they can take time to listen, reflect and gather insights. There is no detailed agenda, no resolutions are proposed, no votes are taken, and no policy statements are issued.[3]

Back in the early days, Bilderbergs were largely responsible for the founding of NATO; today, these super elites convene annually in pursuit of two main goals: consolidating control of the world's money and maintaining military dominance. The first of these goals helped lead to NAFTA, and the latter led to the "forever wars" that pervade our planet. This super elite understands that politics on their level are all but nonpartisan, and history proves this approach successful for them—however disastrous their actions may be for anyone else.

It was the super elites who saw Ronald Reagan as the perfect man for the job of using politics to deploy their plan of economic ruin. Ironically, before he was president of the United States, film star Ronald Reagan was a union man—but not completely. More than that, he served as a member of the board of directors, third vice president, and ultimately, president of the Screen Actors Guild for seven nonconsecutive years.[4] Reagan headed the union, representing Hollywood's biggest film stars during the era when television and the actors appearing on it were seeking compensation equal to what they saw as a significant contribution to the success of the new medium. Reagan fought hard for his fellow actors and, by the time his fifth term was over in 1952, had successfully negotiated residual income for television actors whenever their episodes were rerun. He was unable to do the same for film actors, however. By 1959, when movies were increasingly being telecast, SAG brought Reagan back as president to negotiate for film residuals as well.

With producers refusing to budge, Reagan convinced the union membership they had only one recourse, and so, on March 7, 1960, for the first time in the history of Hollywood, an actor's strike halted all film production. Negotiations resulted in the guaranteeing of telecast residual income for all future films. In addition—in lieu of retroactive film residuals dating back to the television actors' contract—the producers gave SAG a one-time payout, which SAG invested into its first-ever pension and health plans.

While Reagan was effective in fighting for residuals, his tenure at SAG—during which he was a member of the Democratic Party—wasn't without controversy, and hinted at times of the future politician's views. Reagan testified before Senator Joseph McCarthy's House Un-American Activities Committee about "communist-like tactics" within his union as early as 1947, and it was later revealed that, while operating under a code name, he had provided the FBI with names of actors whom he believed were communist sympathizers. By 1966, when the then-former actor was elected Governor of California, Reagan was a Republican through and through, and his support for dissent—including by labor—was at an end. The elites needed a proxy for president in America, and they saw it in Reagan—a Hollywood actor who looked good on TV and was persuadable.

The only things that kept the elites from putting Reagan in office in 1976 were a non-elected, but incumbent president, Gerald Ford, who edged out Reagan in the primary, and the outsider political phenomenon of the Jimmy Carter campaign. In fact, Carter always positioned himself as the outsider challenging the elites. When he was running for governor of Georgia in 1970 against the incumbent, business-minded moderate Carl Sanders, Carter would usually start his speeches off with the same line: "I am basically a redneck," creating a great contrast with the dapperly dressed, then-Governor Sanders. Set aside the career fact, Carter was a nuclear submarine naval officer; he cast a wide *redneck net*, upset Governor Sanders in the election, and kept on running as the peanut farmer with brother Billy and his redneck beer to win the highest office in the land. But even as the ultimate outsider, and by no means a proxy to the elite when he won, the elite would ultimately creep into his presidency, creating the Iran hostage crisis, as would later become evident, according to official documents and stories that surfaced. Here's how the elites come through the back door.

That hostage crisis simmered with the shah of Iran seeking refuge in America. At first, President Jimmy Carter refused him entry; for ten months, he denied the shah admittance because he had hoped to build relations with the new Iranian government and was concerned about staff at the US Embassy in Tehran.[5] Finally, Carter allowed the shah to enter the US for medical treatment, which led to the year-long hostage situation at the Tehran embassy. Although Carter complained about being pressured to admit the shah at the time, it was only years later, in 2019, that documents revealed the extent of the pressure—by no less than the chairman of Chase Manhattan Bank, David Rockefeller, who wanted to allow in one of the bank's most profitable and prestigious clients. The campaign, code name "Project Eagle," involved other elder statesmen including Chase advisory board chairman and former secretary of state Henry A. Kissinger; future Chase chairman and former presidential adviser John J. McCloy; and current and former members of the CIA. Shortly after Carter allowed the shah in, Iranian students took over the Tehran embassy. According to a 2019 article in *The New York Times*:

> The ensuing hostage crisis enabled Ayatollah Ruhollah Khomeini to consolidate his theocratic rule, started a four-decade conflict between Washington and Tehran that is still roiling the region and helped Ronald Reagan take the White House. …
>
> The hostage crisis doomed Mr. Carter's presidency. And the team around Mr. Rockefeller, a lifelong Republican with a dim view of Mr. Carter's dovish foreign policy, collaborated closely with the Reagan campaign in its efforts to pre-empt and discourage what it derisively labeled an "October surprise"—a pre-election release of the American hostages, the papers show.

The Chase team helped the Reagan campaign gather and spread rumors about possible payoffs to win the release, a propaganda effort that Carter administration officials have said impeded talks to free the captives. ...

By 1979, the bank had syndicated more than $1.7 billion in loans for Iranian public projects (the equivalent of about $5.8 billion today). The Chase balance sheet held more than $360 million in loans to Iran and more than $500 million in Iranian deposits.

Mr. Rockefeller often insisted that his concern for the shah was purely about Washington's "prestige and credibility." It was about "the abandonment of a friend when he needed us most," he wrote in his memoirs.[6]

The elites always have an excuse, "too big to fail," or, "best for the country," or, as was the case here, "we started a revolution to help a friend." In reality, it was the usual routine and what elites do best—buy off policymakers to protect their own asses. As you can see with Carter, and I personally experienced with private-equity elites, when they need you, they'll work with you. When they don't need you, they'll throw you under the bus because you're not one of them. That is exactly what happened when the elites went full bore in the 1980 presidential election, when Ronald Reagan was running again and the elites were making their mark.

THESE ARE THE elites I have been talking about, the people who got Ronald Reagan to fire the air traffic controllers, and the same people who got Bill Clinton to pass NAFTA and who got Barack Obama to negotiate the Trans-Pacific Partnership Agreement (TPP). Even after all NAFTA's destruction, they doubled down. It's the same people who finance Big Pharma and dollar-brand retail stores.

The elites are as full a force today as they've ever been. They are directly responsible for the Federal Reserve's decision to prop up the stock market with unlimited socialized spending they call "quantitative easing," which violates every principle of supply and demand and capitalism. Elites invented the phrase "too big to fail" to rescue big banks with taxpayer dollars.

For Bilderbergs, President Trump means something entirely different than he does to intellectual and fiscal elites, as well as Renegades of all stripes. It's doubtful, however, that he's president by their design—especially as Hillary Clinton was an attendee herself in 1997.[7] And while the Renegades played a spoiler role in propelling Trump to the White House, it was the policies of the Bilderberg elite going back forty years that gave rise to their emergence, seemingly from nowhere, to defy intellectual, fiscal, and super elites and upend the rules of their universe.

"Too big to fail" was the "fat lighter" that started the Trump political fire that took over American politics. It sent the message that we will hurt you and drive your livelihoods into the dirt, but we will rob the Federal Treasury to keep the elites from getting hurt.

In 1986, the Bilderberg Group had done its damage

and rearranged our whole industrial output. The Big Four companies that employed the most Americans were General Motors, Sears, Roebuck & Co, IBM, and Ford; today, the largest employers in America are Walmart, Amazon, Kroger, Yum! Brands (the company that operates Taco Bell, Pizza Hut, KFC and WingStreet), and Home Depot.[8]

On the other hand, the financial industry, owned by the super elite, has seen its profits soar over the last forty years, with hedge funds expanding their reach to include credit arbitrage, distressed debt, and fixed income and quantitative strategies— to say nothing of institutional pensions and endowment funds investing in hedge funds in greater numbers. America's second largest export (behind refined petroleum) is now, more than ever, money. And the best way of earning more for elites is finding ways of keeping their wealth capital from trickling down anywhere. Bottom line, Bilderberg elites decided they could not afford a middle class in rural America. The $20-an-hour jobs that Renegades prided themselves on had to go somewhere that the same job would pay $2 an hour.

However, it is fair to point out that the tech sector has done well in some cities post-NAFTA. With an annual median salary of nearly $102,000 in 2019, and a five-year projected growth outlook of 31%, application software developing careers continue to be both lucrative and on the rise for those with computer science degrees. Innovations have made shopping easier, medical procedures less invasive, and information of all stripes more readily accessible. Here's the problem: The tech sector would have a harder chance of capturing older rural America. Prior to that, there was a work ethic and the community cohesiveness required for innovation. NAFTA crushed that community. In fact, NAFTA changed the tech sector in rural America into oil and water.

IN HIS BOOK, *In Defense of Elitism*, Joel Stein writes, very forthrightly, "The main reason Trump won wasn't economic anxiety ... it was that he was an anti-elitist."[9] For many Trump voters, I'm sure this could be the case. But when it comes to the 2.8M Renegade that helped throw the 2016 election, it wasn't the case at all. It wasn't an "economic anxiety" so much as an economic catastrophe that caused those rural Americans to show up from out of nowhere to ultimately cast their "f-u vote" to the Clinton, Obama, and Bush dynasties. You've got to understand what's behind the "f-u" to learn to communicate with these people.

But before the "f-u vote," the country folk of Waycross put their hopes one last time on someone else who, by virtue of his race alone, came across and an outlier—a junior senator from Illinois, Barack Obama.

CHAPTER 10

Desperado

~

BEFORE TRUMP, AMERICA'S working class truly believed Barack Obama, a community organizer turned senator, when he said he would be their champion—the champion of the forgotten man. People who were left out. And he was different, not just because he would be the first Black president, but because they believed the first Black president could understand their condition and would help them. They believed that he would cut the cost of health insurance, make health care available to all, restrict the power of lobbyists, and end the elite raid on the Federal Treasury by those who claimed "too big to fail."

The first Black president in America received 43% of the rural vote in 2008—three points higher than John Kerry had received in 2004.[1] Here we go again—that 2.8 million shows up again at the polls. If they had showed up for Kerry, he would have beat the incumbent, President George W. Bush. By the way, Trump polled three points higher than the pollsters predicted in the 2016 election. So you can see, they voted for Obama first, then they came back and voted for Trump.

Compare those numbers to 2016, when Hillary Clinton would barely hang on to 30% of the rural vote, and the picture gets real clear. *Whoever the 2.8M Renegade turns out for is who wins these elections. They are the game makers.*

The 2.8M Renegade expected to benefit from the Obama mandate, but it turned out to be a huge disappointment for them. And it's about more than race; if it were about race, they would not have voted for him the first time. Instead, the President filled his cabinet with lawyers and bankers and compromised at every turn on the pledges that had earned him their support. After promising to confront growing food monopolies that impacted farmers, no actions were taken—not even after thousands of workers showed up at hearings across the country on the subject.

In his first year in office, President Barack Obama made forty-three trips around the country—only one of them to a rural county in Montana. The following year he visited one hundred four places in America, including six in rural counties, along with vacations in Martha's Vineyard and Maine. If we didn't know better, we could look at 2004 post-election results and say the 2.8M Renegade was not racist against Obama. But Obama's policies were only marginally helpful for rural voters. He didn't lift a finger to help balance the trade agreements. They showed up for him, but he didn't show up for them.

As Bill Bishop wrote in *The Daily Yonder*, a publication by the Center for Rural Strategies:

> *Would it have made a difference if Democrats had shown up in rural America, in person and in policy?*

My guess is that the divisions in the country are deeper than a piece of legislation and a few landings by Air Force One. But the actions by Democrats— rather, their inactions—reinforced the impression that the party didn't care. In a political culture that became increasingly 'us' against 'them.' Democrats were telling those outside the major metropolitan counties that the party wasn't theirs. And so in most of the country, Democrats became the party of "them."[2]

In the COVID-19 relief program known as CARES, Democratic Speaker Nancy Pelosi signed off on the same legislation as Republican leader, Senator Mitch McConnell. What they both got? Campaign financing. CARES was filled with special-interest legislation that would now fund their campaigns in the 2020 election.

Over the eight years that Obama was in office, rural Americans watched as he extended Bush-era tax cuts and failed to close tax loopholes for companies that shipped jobs overseas. They watched the EPA crackdown on the coal mining industry, yet fail to keep their promise to strengthen the communities affected by depleted job opportunities. Mostly, they watched as Obama's promise to help preserve and restore pension protections fell flat, even allowing employee pensions to be cut in bankruptcies.[3] And no one watched this with greater resentment than the 2.8M Renegade voters. Out of high hopes and expectations, they "tuned in" to politics and saw the same thing as what Clinton had done in NAFTA. Even after all the destruction in NAFTA, President Obama backed the Trans-Pacific Partnership Agreement (TPP), which had absolutely no standards for labor or the environment. Global trade can be very positive, but again, you've got to have pro-rata trade agreements.

For many younger Americans, pensions were never to be relied on, which is a tragedy in and of itself—in the early 1990s, about 60% of full-time workers at medium and large companies had pension coverage. By the year Trump took the oath of office, that number had dropped to 24% and was expected to continue to drop.[4]

But retirees in 2016 had put in decades of labor, in which part of every paycheck had gone toward their autumn years. They could only watch as what had been their future savings vanished at the shuttering of businesses—often for the sole purpose of cost-cutting retirement benefits. Still, other retirees found their pensions shifted from traditional benefits to contribution plans like 401(k)s, which took responsibility and investment risk away from employers and placed it on employees—if they had anything left in their paychecks to invest in Wall Street-backed plans.[5] For these older workers, the betrayal by Obama, whose populist platform of "hope" decried such corporate maneuvers and won their vote in 2008, killed them twice.

By 2016, the very youngest of these 2.8M Renegade voters had hit full retirement age, entering senior status—a status that came with grim statistics, and an even grimmer quality of life. With Social Security averaging $14,000 a year for retirees at the time of the election, more and more pensioners found themselves unable to retire, or forced to the brink of poverty—particularly for rural Americans, especially women.[6] With very few, if any, working years ahead of them, they were in a desperate situation and their children were faring worse. This is why they voted for Trump. Public assistance (Social Security, Medicare, food assistance) only went so far. And while the Affordable Care Act had helped lower senior drug costs, between January 2010 and January 2015, forty-four rural hospitals shut down, and by the year Obama left office, twenty-nine million Americans were still without health insurance.[7, 8] This was about half the number than in 2009, but it was a number that still disproportionately affected the rural poor who would gather annually at fairgrounds and parking lots from Appalachia to the Rust Belt for free medical treatment by Remote Area Medical (RAM) caregivers providing medical, vision, and dental services that had been initially established for remote and third-world countries.

The hospital closures had an impact on the working poor in another way, too. In the throes of the meth and opioid crises and with ever-decreasing rehabilitation or treatment options, addicts were finding themselves turning to crime to feed their cravings. This was leading to an increase in rural prison populations at a time when incarceration rates were dropping elsewhere around the country. Obama-era sentencing law revisions had led state and federal prison populations convicted of minor and drug-related crimes to drop in many cities. But in rural America, where bail wasn't always an option, people were increasingly left to languish in overcrowded rural prisons to await trial or serve their sentences—in facilities the *New York Times* would regard as cesspools of dungeons.[9]

Rural America had become a third-world country, a place Washington had forgotten, exemplified in a painting created just two years into Obama's first term. "The Forgotten Man" depicted Obama surrounded by his predecessors, some imploring him to acknowledge a sad man hunched on a bench in the foreground. In the painting, the president ignores everyone, one foot firmly on the US Constitution, the ground around him littered with dollar bills and ragged laws.[10] There was no better depiction of a country run by elites, at the expense of the poor, the unemployed, the addicted.

The aging.

The angry.

Can anybody really ask, "How can they support Trump?" when presidential elections are, by design, a binary choice. It was Trump, and the other choice was who had let them down for forty-five years.

BY ELECTION SEASON 2016, Waycross was dying. Literally. The median household income would prove to be $29,900— 46% below the state average.[11] Almost one out of three of its residents lived below the poverty line.

I had run out of fingers to count the number of friends and neighbors who had fallen so deep into addiction, poverty, illness, or despair—or a combination of those things. Friends with bench warrants. Addicted friends. People just like me with family in prison, or in prison themselves. Neighbors were foreclosing on their family homes. Homeless citizens. Sick friends and dead friends who shouldn't have died.

There were rumors, fast becoming irrefutable, about cancer clusters.[12] They were argued to be the result of shoddy chemical waste removal efforts at abandoned factories, as well as the dumping of chemical waste directly into the soil at Waycross Yards. Added to this, there was the negligence of the long-shuttered Seven Out treatment plant, which left in its wake some 350,000 gallons of toxin-packed waste. Eventually, Ware County, in which Waycross resides, would call nine of Georgia's most contaminated sites their own.

I'd already known from my dad that Waycross had been under close scrutiny for several environmental black eyes. He admitted that he himself saw, more than once, chemicals being drained from railroad cars right onto open ground and into canals. Waycross had also begun accepting toxic potash from Georgia Power and trash from New York and New Jersey.

Our local paper, the *Waycross Journal Herald*, had kept the news of the health threats low on the radar—maybe to avoid panic, given the residents of the town had nowhere to go (no one would buy their property). But they could only keep it secret for so long. In the fall of 2019, the *Herald's* publisher Roger Williams informed the employees that the September 29th edition would be their last edition. The newspaper had been in Waycross for more than 100 years under the Williams family name.

Williams told the employees that the paper had two buyout offers, but both fell through at the last moment. I called Roger—I'd known him for years, as well as his brother Jack, who was editor-in-chief—and left him a message. I offered to buy the paper and keep all his employees hired for one year and said I would give him a royalty of revenue for ten years. I never heard back from him. The next day, Roger Williams killed himself, in his office where I'd left my voicemail.

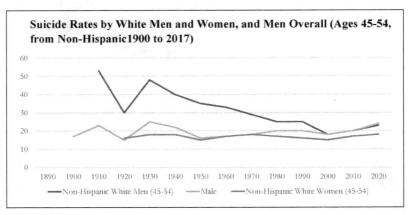

Suicide Rates by White Men and Women, and Men Overall (Ages 45-54, from Non-Hispanic1900 to 2017)

Data built from information obtained from the CDC.[13]

CHAPTER 11

From Rhetoric to Reverie

~

AFTER DECADES OF vanishing unions, vanishing jobs, vanishing health, and vanishing hope, eight years of Obama and partisan gridlock looked like they would morph into more of the same in 2016, with another business-friendly centrist projected to take over the White House. Hillary Clinton was a textbook Washington insider—an Ivy League lawyer who had served as First Lady under Bill Clinton, senator during the administration of President George W. Bush, and Secretary of State under Obama—and in April 2015, she set out to make history as the first woman American president. As she said in her launch speech at a rally in New York City:

> *It's America's basic bargain. If you do your part you ought to be able to get ahead. And when everybody does their part, America gets ahead too. … When President Clinton honored the bargain, we had the longest peacetime expansion in history, a balanced budget, and the first time in decades we all grew together, with the bottom 20% of workers increasing*

their incomes by the same percentage as the top
5%. When President Obama honored the bargain,
we pulled back from the brink of Depression, saved
the auto industry, provided health care to sixteen
million working people, and replaced the jobs we lost
faster than after a financial crash.[1]

In her mind, she had basically written off the towns crushed by NAFTA as "deplorables." It wasn't the people who were deplorable, it was the conditions that she created. She knew America's history—she'd played no small part in writing it—and appealed to an electorate who believed that, with her at the helm, there was nowhere for a recovering economy to go but up. Then, a few short weeks after her announcement, Clinton suddenly found herself facing a primary challenger in self-described "Democratic Socialist" Bernie Sanders, a lifelong activist and populist whose platform focused on social and economic justice. As Sanders said during his campaign speech in his home state of Vermont:

Let me be very clear. There is something profoundly
wrong when the top one-tenth of 1% owns almost as
much wealth as the bottom 90%, and when 99% of
all new income goes to the top 1%. There is something
profoundly wrong when, in recent years, we have
seen a proliferation of millionaires and billionaires
at the same time as millions of Americans work
longer hours for lower wages and we have the highest
rate of childhood poverty of any major country on

earth. There is something profoundly wrong when one family owns more wealth than the bottom 130 million Americans. This grotesque level of inequality is immoral. It is bad economics. It is unsustainable. This type of rigged economy is not what America is supposed to be about. This has got to change and, as your president, together we will change it.[2]

He spoke as he'd spoken all of his career about health care as a human right, the need for a raise in the minimum wage, and his criticism of destructive free trade deals (which Sanders had voted against). Where there had once been "trickle-down economics" theories, Sanders called for a blowing up of the economic dam that has trapped the working-poor Americans. It was, at first, a bold political platform—and in the spring of 2015, the message set traction. There was a political movement in the works.

Local, rank-and-file union chapters increasingly defied their national leadership, who backed Clinton, and gave their support to Bernie Sanders. Despite unfavorable corporate media coverage, his populist message—like Obama's populist message had roused the 2.8M Renegade in 2008—was well-received among the working class and working poor, though not enough to clinch the Democratic nomination. In stark contrast to Clinton's status-quo platform, where the biggest change to the presidency would have been one of gender, Sanders was calling for a revolution that would have upended the status quo everywhere, from Wall Street and the donor class to the Bilderberg elites around the world. The message resonated with progressive activists, but again, not with the 2.8M Renegade who doesn't have time for a revolution.

Sanders was failing to win over either the media or the Democratic delegates—who often pledged their votes to Clinton, even before their state's primaries were held. His message stood in sharp contrast to Hillary Clinton's more incremental status-quo platform. Clinton campaigned—and fundraised—by touting her track record as a DC insider.[3] She pledged to expand the Affordable Care Act, call for a more modest increase to the minimum wage, and denounce the Trans-Pacific Partnership—an unusual move in a candidate who had supported more trade deals than she opposed, including NAFTA, which she had once dubbed the "gold standard." Her war chest groaning from corporate donors, her pledge to address campaign finance reform rang hollow next to Sanders, who famously denounced all super PAC funding, save from the one created and run by the nation's largest union of registered nurses.[4] Clinton rarely ventured into territories where her agenda wouldn't gain support, sending political and celebrity surrogates to campaign on her behalf, and even taking time off in August 2016 from campaigning altogether.[5]

From the Republicans, there was another story coming— and it was declared by candidate Donald Trump:

> *Our country is in serious trouble. We don't have victories anymore. We used to have victories, but we don't have them. When was the last time anybody saw us beating, let's say, China in a trade deal? They kill us. I beat China all the time. All the time. When*

did we beat Japan at anything? They send their cars over by the millions, and what do we do? When was the last time you saw a Chevrolet in Tokyo? It doesn't exist, folks. They beat us all the time. When do we beat Mexico at the border? They're laughing at us, at our stupidity. And now they are beating us economically. They are not our friend, believe me. But they're killing us economically. The US has become a dumping ground for everybody else's problems. Folks, I can take care of it. We can handle it.[6]

To the 2.8M Renegade voters, Trump's rhetoric was a reverie. A nostalgic pride when you didn't have to hide all the problems and everything you had become. From that first day in June 2015, when he rode down his Trump Tower escalator to announce his candidacy, real estate tycoon and television personality Donald Trump seemed to seize on the populist rallying cry and ensuing momentum of Bernie Sanders, tailoring it to fit his own needs. Trump was running a marketing campaign, not a political one, to capture voters. From that day onward, Trump reached out to disillusioned Americans with simple language and emotion-triggering accusations—and always, always, the easily grasped commitment to "Make America Great Again." What could have been a better slogan? Followed by Trump's declaration, "I got your back." Bernie did a better job of identifying problems and solutions for the 2.8M Renegade, but it was all laced around, "Get involved." While Sanders would speak of empowerment through unification, Trump fanned the flames of pointless lies and said, "Let me handle it."

Trump's commoditized message, together with his outrageous refusal to comport himself in the face of his more traditional challengers, provided over a year's worth of bizarre entertainment for watchers of corporate media—with the profits their ratings entailed. Trump's every speech, interview, and tweet was given seemingly wall-to-wall coverage. It provided him billions of dollars in free airtime—and endlessly invaluable opportunities for his message to penetrate. CBS chairman Les Moonves, speaking at a Morgan Stanley Conference in March 2016, went so far as to say the Trump phenomenon might not have been best for America, but that it was "damn good" for his network.[7]

Analysis of major-network campaign coverage in 2015—long before any primaries or caucuses—studied over a thousand minutes of national broadcast television airtime devoted to all the campaigns. Out of that coverage, Donald Trump received 327 minutes—close to one-third of all coverage. Bernie Sanders received just 20 minutes. Hillary Clinton got 121 minutes of campaign coverage, six times that of Sanders. The disparity could best be summed up by *ABC World News Tonight* dedicating 81 minutes of reports to Donald Trump, compared with just 20 seconds for Sanders.[8] Remember: A favorite pastime of the 2.8M Renegade is TV.

With numbers like these—and the theater act he and his crowds provided—Trump pole-vaulted over his challengers, ultimately becoming the Republican nominee. In the absence of any other voice penetrating the pain of rural America—especially after the contentious Democratic convention declared Clinton their candidate—Trump's message took. It was populism on a different scale, championing the attendees of his rallies, which took on the form of sporting events, complete with tailgate parties and team colors—the red and white of Team MAGA.

The night before the election in Pennsylvania, Trump's message had been honed down to a philosophy that was felt all the way to Waycross:

> *We get nothing. This will all change, folks. It will change very, very fast. And it will be—it will be a two-lane highway, maybe a one—maybe one lane for a little while, but one way coming here, but just for a little while. We have to catch up, this is a lot of years. A lot of years we've been abused by people who don't know what they're doing. A lot of years, we've been abused by stupid politicians, very stupid politicians ... supports totally open borders. There goes your country. And your plan gives your Social Security benefits—you know, she wants to give them to illegal immigrants.*
>
> *We will stop illegal immigration, deport all criminal aliens, and dismantle every criminal gang and cartel corrupting our citizens ...*
>
> *Get your family, get your friends. No matter what you do, you've got to get out and vote.*
>
> *The whole world is laughing at us.*

Yet when November 8, 2016 finally arrived, *everyone knew* Hillary was supposed to win. The only unpredictable factor was by how wide a margin.[9] That day, 2.8M Renegade revenge began but nobody saw it coming as giddy Democrats flocked to their polling stations to elect America's first woman president and defeat the reality TV star Donald Trump.

News outlets breathlessly recorded the events of the day, complete with cosplaying women and even babies showing up at the polls in their Hillary-style pantsuits and pearls.[10, 11] Parties were planned for the next day where crowds could gather outside Trump properties to point and laugh at the defeated candidate in "a display of old-fashioned, post-election mockery in the face" of Trump's crudeness and rudeness toward the Democratic candidate.[12]

And then—the returns started coming in. All across the map, Trump was gaining electoral votes, flipping states so traditionally blue that Hillary Clinton had barely bothered to stump in them—particularly the upper Midwest states of Wisconsin, Iowa, Ohio, and Pennsylvania, where she sent the likes of Joe Biden, Bernie Sanders, and even her husband, former President Bill Clinton, to campaign in her stead.

Out of 676 counties in swing states that had delivered for Barack Obama twice, 209 voted for Trump that day. Out of the 207 counties that Obama had won once, Clinton won only thirteen. In Ware County, Clinton received only 3,440 votes (28%) compared to Trump's 8,513 votes (69%).[13] By the next morning, Hillary Clinton had conceded, leaving supporters and pundits in a fog trying to figure out how their predictions had been so inaccurate.

It was when pollsters studied electoral data in the rural areas that a pattern emerged— Renegade revenge.[14] Unprecedented Republican support was detected in rural precincts across the country. What happened? In the end, political statisticians would conclude that an increase in reported voters from 2012—some 4.6 million people—played a large role in polling miscalculations in 2016.[15] Out of that number, 3.7 million new voters—*over 85%*—were sixty-five years of age and older, 2.8 million of them non-Hispanic whites. More and more studies along income and class lines would add up to one unmistakable conclusion—the 2.8M Renegade vote had handed the presidency to Donald Trump.[16]

A YEAR LATER, in November 2019, I went home for Thanksgiving. The Big Star grocery was long gone. So were the Winn-Dixie, Pick 'n Save, and Piggly Wiggly. Nothing remained but dollar-brand stores and fast food chains.

Growing up on Swamp Road we, like many, would have had a traditional Southern Thanksgiving meal—turkey, ham, pecan pie made with fall pecans picked up from the eight trees in Grandmama's yard, collard greens, lima beans, lady peas that had been stored fresh in the freezer, cornbread dressing, and pan cornbread. After lunch, we would have gone deer hunting and wandered across the lowlands of the swamp. That night we would have gone into the swamp—coon hunting and chasing after dogs.

Instead, I picked up plates from Cracker Barrel and found myself in the aftermath of an economic war zone, a crater where Waycross was almost like a place where people went to die. To get it over with.

It's worse than walking through the urban blight of Chicago or even Harlem thirty years ago.

Here's why: Isolation.

Urban decay at least has density, and is why an area like Harlem can reinvent itself—it's harder to ignore. Waycross is flat, wide, and is overshadowed by an eerie emptiness: "Where have all the people gone?" Even with the drudgery of stats that point to a decline well below that of a third-world country, with the lack of community and citizens, it makes the chances of a comeback so less likely.

My cousin's plans for Thanksgiving afternoon were to drink Jack Daniels and watch Westerns. I was invited, but decided to stay with Dad and talk politics.

About then.

About today.

About tomorrow.

CHAPTER 12

The Solution

~

GUARANTEED MINIMUM INCOME has to be front and center of any strategy to solve the rural rot, and reveries have to be replaced by real jobs and hope for the future. I say "real" because providing people with training for jobs that don't exist doesn't cut it. You can't wait on private enterprise to make the first move. The government is obligated to redistribute the wealth back into the hands of a working middle class, so a great start is a tax on Wall Street transactions. I'm not saying give away money free, but use it to get back to people "earning" again—and with all the human and community dignity that comes with it. Any comprehensive employment job-training act should include a job you are training for, doing, and getting paid for today. It goes back to culture: a job and being left alone. Truth, the 2.8M Renegade don't even mind if they don't like the job. They just do it. President Franklin D. Roosevelt was known as the first big spender on government programs, but the genius of his vision was to structure those programs around the Work Progress Administration (WPA). Later, we had earned income tax credits, which were, again, based around work and earnings.

The great news is that the 2.8M Renegade is not afraid of work; they are very smart and efficient when it comes to learning new skills on the job. The necessary, massive job creation projects designated for rural areas could revolve around green energy and paid apprenticeships. One million new jobs at a salary of $48,000 would be lower than what we have spent on wars since NAFTA passed. The elite donor class makes a lot of money off of wars. It's why we have had so many last so long since NAFTA passed; they saw they could get their way at home, so why not abroad as well?

The only way the elite will agree to this is to let them make money off of rural renewal. Government could guarantee the investments like it does the FDIC. It will have to be as aspirational and creative as The New Deal, so it could be called simply be called The Get Real Rural Deal, where the government guarantees a minimum return, if needed.

If we've had enough and don't want the elite donor class to make money off the massive restoration and rule the roost yet again, then we have to cure the real rot, the political industrial complex of campaign bribes for outcomes on legislation, judiciary proceedings, and decisions and executive orders from the White House to the city council.

Here is the reality: When serious and citizen-minded FDA officials had the pharmaceuticals industry caught on tape for illegally pushing opioids, the top brass at FDA called off and out the front-line investigators and made them destroy the taped evidence. President Obama, Mitch McConnell, and Nancy Pelosi signed legislation to weaken the FDA investigative body so it could not be repeated. Truth be told, this is baby stuff compared what is going on at the Pentagon, banks, and State Department every day. I give President Trump credit for reaching out directly to the North Korean leader and bypassing State Department bureaucracy who, for twenty years, sabotaged talks to ensure the military industrial complex kept its bases running in the Korean Peninsula.

Before Trump and after Trump, America no longer has a "republic" for the common good, which Merriam-Webster defines as "a government in which supreme power resides in a body of citizens entitled to vote and is exercised by elected officers and representatives responsible to them and governing according to law." It was and is still owned lock, stock, and barrel, by the elites who can start wars, who can extinguish communities, and who figured out how to own both bookends of Washington, DC. The mainstream media has done a 24/7 job on the shortcomings of Trump, but they paint the picture as if everything was perfect before Trump. They, too, have a lot of responsibility to bear for letting it go on for forty-five years. However, big networks are owned by big elites. However, we cannot say we were not warned.

Walking out of the Constitutional Convention of 1787, where our republic was born, our eldest founding father Benjamin Franklin sprinkled a heavy dose of skepticism on our newly formed government as, "a republic, if you can keep it." Here is how we reclaim it and keep it for another one hundred years.

1. No bailouts unless voted on by the American public.
2. Every corporation greater than $1 billion in revenue pays a minimum of 10% in taxes.

3. Certified electronic voting implemented in all fifty states.

4. End all congressional pension and retirement plans.

5. Companies less than ten years old and have at least 10% growth per year have their first $1 million owed in taxes waived.

6. Federal lobbying is outlawed within five hundred miles of Washington DC.

7. Appointed expert counsel will approve all military contracts and manage bidding process.

8. Americans have access to the same medical plan as Congress.

9. Congressional campaigns cannot spend more than the aggregated total salary of the term.

10. Start-ups pay no tax on the first $1 million earned in revenue.

11. No tax cuts implemented unless approved by American voters.

12. All trade deals rescinded unless they meet the minimum US environmental standards.

Personal Reveries—Picking Up Pecans (Pee Cans)

~

OFTEN, I THINK I am still the boy who overjoyed Grandmama and Daddy by filling grocery bags full of pecans (or as we would say, *pee cans*), instead of sticks and leaves, at age five. I was assigned to the task while Grandmama was doing chores and always moving. But while I overperformed at picking up pecans, I had no access to preschool, kindergarten, or even bedtime stories.

I started my first day of first grade—my first day in any classroom setting—not knowing how to read or write. Sitting there in the front row, where my brother Kenny had placed me as Daddy had instructed (like that was going to be the difference-maker), I was scared to death. And that feeling was accurate: Almost right away, the teacher, Ms. Jones, separated those of us who didn't know how to read or write into a separate group known as "Group 5." There were three of us who wore the Group 5 label.

By the fourth grade, I had caught up with the rest of my class. Years later, when the time came, I was accepted into West Georgia College. By the way, I had only heard about the SAT test on the Friday afternoon before the final one was administered for the next year's college admissions. West Georgia was considered a *redneck* college by many because most of the student body were first-generation college students coming from working families, but West Georgia had three tremendous advantages that not only saved me, but also shaped me to win over elites. The first was that the school had built out a world-class English department (done so because rednecks, myself included, had heavy slang and double negatives). I was totally caught off guard by Dr. Martha Saunders, my English composition professor, when she told me I was in grave danger of not making it out of remedial English. I'm grateful for the school's English department because it helped me quickly course correct and move ahead. The second advantage was that Newt Gingrich had taught at West Georgia before being elected to Congress, and he'd left the history and political science departments with a rich legacy. Finally, the third advantage of attending West Georgia was that it had a nationally renowned debate coach, Dr. Chester Gibson, whose teams routinely beat the likes of Harvard and Dartmouth. During the first quarter of my freshman year, I took Dr. Gibson's speech class. Drawl and all, he offered me a scholarship slot on his debate team. These three advantages set me on a path that I would remain on for the rest of my university days.

I worked my ass off and was eventually accepted to Emory University's MBA program. I was filled with trepidation over competing with students from the top schools in the country—Harvard, Yale, Chapel Hill, and the like. On the first day of class, the dean came in and announced that he was particularly proud of the undergraduate academic achievements and institutions of the class, then he asked each of us to stand and say where we were from and which college we had graduated from.

In a class of forty-seven students, I was third from last in line—alphabetically behind all the Ivy League schools. When the student in front of me stood up, gave the Nixon wave, and said he was from the University of Georgia, the class boiled over with laughter. Then it was my turn. I stood and said, "Waycross, West Georgia College." In the deafening silence that followed, you could almost hear their thoughts: *How did they let a redneck in here?* To make matters worse, I still had the Waycross nasal twang embedded in every syllable.

Although the first month at Emory was a little rough, the school changed my life. After a couple of months, I was pleasantly surprised to find myself at the front of the class in writing and creative thinking.

Outhouses Outlast Memories

AS FAR AS social status goes, Swamp Road was so far in the sticks it was at the bottom of the *redneck* totem pole. It did have one great advantage that I learned very early—not to prejudge other people because of their economic circumstances. I was around age ten when the Beaches, a family of five, moved into a rental owned by JC Lewis. They arrived one day in a car with all their belongings, and it wasn't long before I really began to understand that what matters about people is who they are, not where they come from.

It never really bothered us that Grandmama's house only had one closet-style bathroom that served three generations under that one roof—at least it was indoor plumbing, unlike the house about three hundred yards down the road that only had an outhouse. It was owned by JC Lewis, who bought the land after my Uncle Kenny tragically died in a freak motorcycle accident immediately after arriving home without a scratch from World War II. Mr. Lewis bought the land from my grandfather only after he pledged not to turn it into a junkyard—which, of course, he did in less than a year. He also bought and moved three condemned houses from town and made them Swamp Road frontage property. Those shacks made him a swamplord in his own right, collecting between $28 and $40 per month, per house. Lewis' landlord hopes were set back by his two sons, who shacked up in the two houses with indoor bathrooms, leaving him with only one house to rent—the one with no bathroom.

Families would come and go in that house, and many of the children became our playmates and friends. One of those families was the Beaches. The father of the family was older and seemed distracted and distant, but always very polite. The mom was much younger and mentally challenged; she was mother to the youngest child and stepmother to the two older teenagers—who were only a couple of years older than she. The oldest child, Joseph, who was around my age, read a lot of books and was a straight-A student. He was often teased for sharing clothes with his sister, but my brother Kenny always saved a seat for Joseph next to him on the school bus.

I was amazed at Joseph's knowledge of space, forests, and then girls (which became important as I got older). In a country home, nudity, sex, or even kissing were forbidden topics of discussion, so Joseph's knowledge of subjects outside my redneck orbit struck my curiosity. Although Joseph was surrounded by poverty and mental instability, he was not a redneck. He had a sophisticated intellect, was always reading, and was always very courteous when my grandmother made a meal for him. Through Joseph, I began to understand that what matters about people is what's on the inside.

Around age sixteen, as I turned the corner toward adulthood, I was no longer satisfied with the pace of life on the swamp. I give a lot of credit to Joseph for lifting my mind to higher places, for helping me to understand that there was a world outside Swamp Road. Walking through the dark swamps at night, I dreamt of walking the big-city streets where corn doesn't grow.

Forgive and Forget

I THINK MY grandmother was kind and forgiving of her daughter-in-law, my mother, because she knew there was another side to the story; my mother, Barbara Pardon, was barely fifteen when she had my brother Kenny, and I'm sure was young and confused. She had two more children before she reached age twenty. I have never known much about my mother's family, just that they were hell raisers from the word *go*. I often heard from others that our mother was "a looker," and "here for the party," but growing up, we did not see her very often.

In their mid-teens, Kenny and Beth reconnected with her with high hopes that soon faded to disappointment. But we remember fondly the visits of her sister, our Aunt Francis, who brought some glitz and glamour to Swamp Road. She became a model in magazines and would visit us when she came back to her hometown, Waycross. Grandmama loved her and doted on her. She was beautiful and wore sunglasses, which we didn't even know existed until we saw them on her. She even bought me a pony named Trigger.

However, those visits came to an end when our dad married Mary.

At first it was a delight. I was five and remember the first day quite well. Beth was ten, and Kenny was eleven when Mary showed up at Grandmama's house as Daddy's new wife. Beth and Kenny—overjoyed that we had a mother in the house—jumped up and down for joy on the beds in the back room, and Grandmama welcomed her just as she had us.

But soon it was apparent that Mary was smart and with a medically-induced mental madness to save every penny, which later we discovered was to give to our younger brother Matt. Mary's dream was to have money so Matt did not have to work. He was born soon after she and Daddy married. By the way, we were never told the date, day, or any details of the wedding ceremony; to this day, we're unsure if there was one. Mary had known my mother and was jealous of her beauty, and soon it was apparent that she was jealous of a lot of things. Once Matt was born, Mary gained full leverage over Daddy, who turned away from the rest of us emotionally and never really said a word when Mary built a wall between him and us. Basically, it became Mary, Matt, and Daddy on one side and Grandmama, Kenny, Beth, and me on the other. I think our dad was trying to keep the peace and avoid another divorce. It was the toughest on Kenny because he was the most outgoing and athletic; he played sports and could ride any horse bareback at full speed. Dad had been made a train conductor at the railroad and was our hero when he arrived home in that uniform.

Mary rid us of everything we loved—our horses, ball gloves, birthday parties, friends, and family—and made us work for the things we wanted. At age ten, Kenny and I were working in the tobacco fields, and at fifteen, Beth was a cashier at Pick 'n Save. We were working-class folks from a young age.

Despite the fact that our lives felt more deprived, Daddy was doing very well with his job on the railroad, and eventually he and Mary built a brick house three hundred feet away from my grandmother's. It would be considered modest pretty much anywhere, except on Swamp Road. Yet it was a bad day by all accounts when we moved from Grandmama's house into Daddy and Mary's neighboring house. Grandmama did what she could to shield us from Mary's deeply explosive ways, gathering us outside behind the barn or washhouse to tell us Mary needed to see a doctor and to forgive her. Later, Grandmama moved in with us in the "new house" to look after us and save us from the daily family hell. Even after living through the Great Depression, two world wars, life with my grandfather, and the untimely death of a son, she was still willing to put up with

Mary—sometimes I think Grandmama was put on this earth to be tortured. But I only heard her complain one time, when she told my dad, "Mary mistreats the children."

But family hell had been part of our lives for generations. To his credit, it was Granddad who instructed my dad to go pick us up from the projects. Still, no doubt he would be jailed today for the way he abused his family, especially his son, my daddy, who, after standing up to him one day as a kid, ended up being choked into unconsciousness—coming around only to be warned that the next time, he wouldn't be so lucky. I am told he was mean to everyone, except me. I still remember him chewing Red Man tobacco while milking the cow before heading out on his dairy route to area stores, with me riding on the front seat of the truck next to him holding on to a sixteen-ounce RC Cola from Haines Grocery, a filling station that sold milk and bread.

Daddy and Yellow Dog Democrats

DADDY WAS A Yellow Dog Democrat—he would vote for a yellow or sick dog before he would vote for a Republican. The rest of the South had been Yellow Dog Democrats until the civil rights vote, when Lyndon Johnson said he had lost the South for generations. Truth was, he did lose the South—but not my father, who was well read, smart, and not preoccupied with religion or entertainment of hunting, fishing, and drinking. He'd been scarred by an event that happened in his childhood during the Great Depression. His father, my grandfather, turned to drinking and my grandmother couldn't scrape up the money for his school lunch, so the teachers made him stay in the classroom while everybody else went and ate. Dad believed in a social safety net, and our dinner conversations often centered on why Democrats were so great and Republicans so bad. In Daddy's mind, Republicans were those people who told him he couldn't eat, and didn't deserve a school lunch.

When Kenny was in Ms. Edith Ponder's class, she had every student stand up and say who their parents were voting for in the presidential election with Richard Nixon and Hubert Humphrey. And if you did not know, you had to go home and ask. Four or five students immediately stood up in a row and said "Richard Nixon." Kenny stood up and said, "I know for sure my daddy is voting for George McGovern." The teacher gave Kenny a long lecture on why his dad was so wrong and how the Democrat would cause communism to come to America. It unusually caught my attention at age five and I still remember it.

Dad remained a liberal Democrat, whereas 98% of everybody else in town was a Primitive Baptist right-wing believer, especially after the fight for civil rights took hold and Jerry Falwell passionately introduced religion as a mainstay to politics.

Oh' Glory

DADDY AND MARY were not church-goers, though Grandmama was a believer in Jesus and prayed every night. Her Christian principal: Pass judgement on nobody. Grandmama, Kenny, Beth, and I rode the church bus every Sunday morning and night, and every Wednesday night. Daddy was, most of the time, gone on a railroad run and Grandmama told us to leave Mary alone. So we all caught the bus together, sometimes three times per week. It is far worse to ride a church bus when you had two cars in the driveway, as we did, than to ride when you had no transportation, as was the case with our fellow passengers on the bus. There were also nine or ten mentally disturbed people the driver would pick up at a local foster home.

To this day, whenever I hear the song, "I'll Fly Away," I remember the driver singing it over and over on Sunday nights to keep the mentally challenged riders entertained on the way back from church to their home. He would drop them off first, but it was still a forty-five minute ride because he always stopped at the Okefenokee Grocery where the church bought everybody an Icee.

One day, Beth came to Grandmama crying because Daddy had told her she was not old enough to go out with a boy. As usual, Grandmama didn't say anything negative about Daddy, but she solved the problem for Beth when she said, "Invite him to ride the church bus with us Sunday evening and you all can sit together." Although Beth doubted he would, the young man named Steve was in the third seat from the front on the right side of the bus when Beth boarded and quickly he asked her to sit down. That night, coming home on the bus after we had stopped for our Icee, Beth and Steve were sitting close together. Grandmama was in the front seat and she turned and smiled when she saw my sister laughing as we rode along.

Kenny, Beth, and I had some of our best memories on that church bus.

Bruno and Burglar

DESPERATION CAN MAKE people do desperate things. One night in that house on Swamp Road, we heard the back-door steps creak and then the latch on the screen door rattle. We all ran to Grandmama, who told us someone was on the back porch. As we latched onto her legs, she made it back to Daddy's room and took the pistol out of the drawer. Then we saw the latch on the back door move and rattle. Kenny, Beth, and I, none older than age nine, started crying and Grandmama huddled us in the comer of the living room. She then walked toward the door and in a raised but confident voice said, "Let Daddy through with the gun!" Suddenly, we could hear the back-door steps complain as someone ran across them and out the back screen door.

Kenny called our Uncle Buddy and asked him to come down as someone was trying to break in on the back porch. A few minutes later, we were all relieved when Buddy's headlights hit the inside of our house. Grandmama told us to stay inside and let Buddy come in. Buddy had his brother Wayne with him and both flew down the steps and started circling our house with rifles, opening the barn doors, and shooting bullets into the air. About fifteen minutes later, we all walked out to the front yard where a fine pelt of dew had already fallen; the swamp air was always thick with water. With a light mist trailing the air, Buddy had a serious look on his face and showed us where someone had cut a hole in the screen door—cigarette butts that were smoldering on the wooden doorsteps. He said, "Somebody was trying to break into here. I bet with your daddy's truck not here, they thought nobody was home."

"I wish we could have been here a little earlier so we could have shot his ass," Wayne said.

Buddy told Grandmama that he would come back first thing in the morning and fix the screen door if my daddy was not back by then. Grandmama thanked them and we three kids just marveled in their presence and security as well as in the glee of having company—even if it were under night patrol circumstances.

"Call us if you hear anything else," Buddy said, "but I'm sure he heard those bullets so he won't be coming back."

As they drove off, Grandmama took us all back in the house and told us it was time to get to bed. Then she said, "Well, *bless kaydee*, I got to close your daddy's window." The window was level with the bed, so to reach the window sill, she bent over and put her feet under the bed. That's when Grandmama's feet felt flesh and bone.

"That man is under your daddy's bed!" she yelled.

But before we could come out of the back bedroom, our German Shepard Bruno ran out from under the bed, through Grandmama's legs, and to the front door to be let outside. We finally realized that when the dog heard all the rifle shots, he must have run inside and hidden. We all belly laughed when we realized that, for a moment, Grandmama thought Bruno was the monster man. We went to sleep with the laughter and love of our grandmother talking to us from her room into our back bedroom where I slept in a bed with my brother that was flush to my sister's mattress, because there was barely enough space in the room.

Later that night, I heard the back door open and, too frightened to call out, I gasped for air. When I happily realized it was Daddy opening the door, returning home from the train yard with his work satchel in hand, I rolled over and went back to sleep.

The next morning, Daddy got up to see us to before we caught the school bus and we told him all about the events from the night before. Daddy told us that that hole in the screen door had been their awhile and that somebody might had run out of gas and needed help. But that morning, Daddy drove up to Frank Eldridge's hardware store and bought a deadbolt for the back door and a new screen for the back porch door.

Kenny, Beth, and I were easily scared at night by sounds or dreams. We later surmised a lot of it was most likely due to our mother leaving us alone in the projects all night as children, which was the main reason the judge had allowed our dad to take us from her. My sister has told me how, as a five-year-old, she would wake up at night hearing me crying and would find her way to the kitchen, get a bottle of milk, and funnel it through the crib to my three-month-old toddler mouth. My mother would prepare the milk before she went to work at the twenty-four-hour Waycross Café, and she would always wait until we were asleep before leaving the house.

Growing up in the swamp is one thing, but the children of the NAFTA fallout have it much harder. For one thing, these days, in addition to caring for younger ones, they often find themselves caring for their opioid-addicted parents.

Mr. Misty

DADDY TOLD US we were all going out to eat for Kenny's high school graduation. He said we would go somewhere like Captain Joe's. Daddy said he would "mark off" at work, meaning he would take the day off and be marked "off" on the dispatch board to make sure he could be home. It was rare for Daddy to ever miss work, so we were excited for the day to come.

After Mary moved in, Daddy had little time to recognize anything Kenny did, and he had started getting into trouble, giving her even more reasons to alienate him. The graduation was on a Friday evening at 7 p.m. at Memorial Stadium in Waycross. Around 4 p.m., Daddy told Grandmama we all needed to get dressed because we would leave as soon as Mary got home from work, before 6 p.m. By 5 p.m., we were all dressed, including Kenny, who had to leave before us by 5:30 p.m. For the first time in eight years, it was Grandmama, Daddy, Kenny, Beth, and me sitting in the living room—laughing and talking and celebrating Kenny's accomplishment. We were reminiscing about some of the psycho acts of Kenny's teacher, and how his antics made her act even worse. We also talked about Kenny's favorite teacher, Ms. Penn, in whose class he received high grades all year.

Then we heard the door open—it was Mary. She walked into the living room, saw us sitting there enjoying ourselves, and blurted out to Daddy, "You are not going to spend money at a restaurant." She then angrily huffed down the hall, saying, "I'm not going anywhere," went into the bedroom and slammed and locked the door.

Kenny stood up and said, "Daddy, I need to get going."

The rest of us were sad, but didn't say anything; we were used to Mary. Daddy went down the hall and into his and Mary's bedroom, and at around 6 p.m., Grandmama said through their door, "Willie Clyde, we need to go." Daddy came out of the room and said, "Let's load up the car." Beth asked if Mary was coming, but Daddy said he didn't think so; she ended up staying home with our youngest brother. The rest of us got in the car and hardly said a word on the way to the stadium. Daddy's attitude went from being proud of Kenny to being distant and maybe even displeased for having to go with all of us. After the ceremony, we stopped at the Dairy Queen where we each got a Mr. Misty, which only made Mary cuss when we got home. The next morning, Beth went to work at her job at Pick 'n Save, I started my job cropping tobacco, and Kenny packed up and moved in with my cousin Walter.

What I Learned About Business as a South Georgia Bottom Fisher

WHEN I TELL people that the first business lesson I ever learned was with Louisiana Pinks, they often think I was in the nail polish or lipstick businesses, or maybe rose bushes. Sorry, not at the age of fifteen, living in rural southern Georgia. I was in none of those businesses. I was selling worms.

A Louisiana Pink is a premium live worm that is an excellent bottom-fishing bait in rivers and ponds. They are bigger and pinker than earthworms, and their real advantage is that they stay alive longer on the hook, which attracts larger catfish and bream. But, boy, they came at a price. Thirty or forty years ago, they cost about 10 to 15 cents each—compared to regular earthworms, which were basically free.

When our local bait and tackle store Winges went up on the price to 20 cents a piece, or $4 a box, my Uncle Buddy and I decided to dive into the Louisiana Pink business. We quickly learned a lesson I would long remember: all businesses are technical in nature, no matter how simple they may seem. Do you know your business? Do you have resident knowledge of the ins and outs of the business that others don't have? I have seen, over and over again, that the answers to those questions are among the strongest indicators of success.

Sometimes we jump in too quick because the business is a passion or a passing fancy, which is what it was for Uncle Buddy and me. When Winges raised its prices and we got market intelligence that the store was buying them for $2.25 per box, we saw dollar signs—never mind that we didn't know anything about worm-bed habitation or whether a premium product like this might require extra care. We saw those dollar signs again when the worm distributor told us he would sell us the worms for the same price he was selling them to Winges. As we posted our sign—"Louisiana Pinks $3 per box"—we figured this was just too easy.

Excited, we didn't give much thought to the first investment we needed to make: a refrigerator to keep the worms cool. We filled it with our first order, 50 boxes. Three nights later, our worm fever began to cool.

We had only sold two boxes—to my cousin, Walter—and we had already had to throw out five boxes. We were puzzled.

Every worm in these boxes was what we called graveyard dead, not a single wiggle from any of them. This was especially worrisome because we knew Winges worms were always moist, brightly pink and balled together in lively knots. Our worms looked more pitiful each day.

We sped over to Winges to check out their cooler, and we quickly realized our problem: the refrigerator. Ours was too cold, even after we moved the thermostat to the highest setting. This was a setback, but we didn't panic. We pooled our money and bought a used cooler so that our Pinks could reside comfortably in cool air, not cold. We were optimists by nature, and we were feeling pretty good about our ability to adjust and learn.

That evening, things got out of hand again. I have noticed that, whenever people don't know what they are doing in a business, bad luck seems to show up at every turn. Right before closing, two well-known fishermen stopped by and asked for four boxes of Pinks. This is what we wanted to hear, of course, and you might say were tickled pink—until I broke off the key trying to unlock the cooler door.

With our faces red, we asked them when they were going fishing. They told us the next afternoon, so we suggested that they come back the next day. Uncle Buddy assured them we would get the cooler fixed and have their worms ready first thing in the morning. We waited all day, but they never came back. Of course, "waiting" is what you do when you don't know what to do.

Next, we discovered that our worms were disappearing. At night we would count twenty in a box, and the next morning we might have sixteen or fifteen. Apparently, they were eating each other. We were so spooked and puzzled that we made the decision to go back to Winges and try to talk to the owner. He had a relatively large operation: full-service gas station, beer and wine, snacks, full lineup of rods and reels, with a large assortments of tackle and five different live baits, including shrimp, minnows and, of course, Louisiana Pinks.

Interrupting him as he hustled around his business, we explained that our worms were dying and pleaded with him to take a look. He nodded yes, started walking toward our truck, and said, "I heard something about you all selling worms out there." Believe me, he had not lost nearly as much sleep as we had. He opened a box and threw the dirt and all inside the bed of our truck. He picked up a handful of worms and let the dirt sift through his fingers. He pulled the worms apart.

As Uncle Buddy and I stood in dead cold silence, he started rattling off directives: You need to punch an extra hole in the top of that cartoon—you need five holes, not four. And your cooler needs a light mist—this dirt is too dry. And you're overfeeding them, they need to burrow for their food. He went on and on until he finally said, "I wish you all would have asked me before you started. I carry those Pinks because nobody else around these parts will. I make a little money on them, but not much—just like I do with fishing licenses." And then he used a phrase that I had never heard before: "They are more or less loss-leaders."

Uncle Buddy gave away the cooler and every live Louisiana Pink in it. But I've kept the lessons I learned to this day. You need to know the business. You also have to be able to attract others who know the business.

You have to ask yourself, what is your personal brand? If you are an overachiever, you are going to attract overachievers.

If you are a partier, you are most likely to attract partiers, which may not be bad for some businesses.

Be careful about listening to all of the talk about following your passion. I would say your knowledge about the business beats passion every day of the week. No matter how much you love the business, you probably can't afford on-the-job training.

Finally, ask around. Ask other business owners. They tend to be surprisingly open about sharing the challenges they face, and believe me, every industry has problems and hurdles.

The best way to change an industry and create a new market is to know what is working now and which customers are being underserved. If you don't know that, go fishing.

Waffle House Shows Atlanta How
to Handle a Snowstorm

The New York Times

[Originally published in The New York Times on February 17, 2014 and reprinted with permission.]

ATLANTA'S SECOND SNOW jam of 2014 shut down practically every business of every size in the city. But I don't think we can entirely blame Mother Nature or even the governor this time for the lost revenue and customers that we will all be adding up at the end of the month.

In some ways, I think we closed the door in our own faces. Despite the dire forecasts, on Tuesday we basically had a rain shower. But because of the warnings and the disastrous experience of Snow Jam 1, most businesses made the decision on Monday—long before the "storm" hit—to send everyone home. And yet, while most companies retreated, one business held its ground. No, it was not a giant like FedEx, UPS or AT&T. No new legends like Pony Express were made here. The one company I saw that had the winning spirit was Waffle House, a regional restaurant chain and cultural icon with more than 1,700 locations. If you are familiar with Waffle House, you know that unusual things tend to happen there, whether it is a Waffle House wedding, Kid Rock getting into a fight, or terrorists gathering to plot, but the organization stood tall in the snow.

In fact, the morning after, as I sat in a Waffle House enjoying the famous "scattered, smothered and covered" hash browns and talking to a waitress named Irene and a manager named Bob, I learned that not one Waffle House had closed for the second storm. Both Bob and Irene were smiling, their eyes shining. They were happy warriors at work, and I quickly found out why.

As they strolled back and forth with food, they talked about how the restaurant bought up hotel rooms next to the Waffle House so employees would have a place to stay. On Monday, Bob said they spent the day coordinating so that employees who had four-wheel-drive vehicles could pick up employees who did not, including Irene. "There he came, right through the snow," she said, proudly. Somehow, her smile made the cheese grits taste even better.

As I watched this Waffle House turn its customers into raving fans, I thought about all the doom and gloom I had heard on Monday about why businesses should close. But Waffle

House stayed open for the same reason most businesses chose to close. It followed the lead of management. Waffle House acted as if it wanted to stay open, so the team bonded and got it done, despite the looming threat of a storm that CNN labeled "a catastrophic event with historic, crippling consequences." Waffle House won with a sense of purpose that will do that company a lot of good for a long time to come.

Can you imagine a management consultant or motivational speaker trying to tell this team how to bond, lead, and grow? The management teams—like mine!—that made the decision on Monday to close on Tuesday wanted to act as if they cared. So they retreated. When I told my team to come in on Tuesday, I heard horror stories about the previous snowstorm, and the risk that we might all get caught at work with no way home. It was as if I was putting work over their well being—set aside the fact a snowflake had yet to fall within a thousand-mile radius.

But sending employees home means you care. "Go home" is a quick, easy, and cheap way for managers to get a hug and be a five-second hero. So we all joined the herd and adopted the go-home mentality—and the roads became crammed—just as they were during the first storm. Meanwhile, Waffle House figured out how to run away from the herd and serve both its customers and employees.

It is rarely clear precisely what gets people to join together and connect as a team. But we do know this: You can't fake it with easy yeses to suck up to the team—a fool's errand every time. We have to snap out of this in Atlanta.

Will my employees remember that I let them go home early? There might be five seconds of goodwill there.

Will Irene remember that four-wheel-drive cutting across her neighborhood to pick her up? I'm guessing it could be up there somewhere close to her wedding day.

While Waffle House will remember that its little yellow light shone brightly in the snows of Atlanta, the rest of us will remember a lot of gloom, doom and boredom.

Waycross Crosses Wall Street

THE SO-CALLED dot-com crash of 2000 actually ended up helping the company I'd founded, and made us look like a star in the eyes of Wall Street. Prior to the crash, Wall Street was hot for taking unprofitable tech-based companies public, shifting the risk of money-losing ventures from themselves to the public, and walking away with tens of millions in fees from shady IPOs (initial public offerings) before moving on to the next loser. After the crash, with big failures revealing the dodgy IPO scheme, Wall Street approached my company, STI because we were not only growing as fast as their fantasy failures managed to in the short term, but we were also creating profits, and had been doing so for a long time. Wall Street pushed hard for me to make STI a publicly owned company.

It was an attractive proposition. A financial windfall would be a total validation for a swamp boy. Growing up, Kenny, Beth, and I missed a lot of things in our childhood; I was determined to show the world and Mary and Daddy for the three of us.

So we did what's called the "Wall Street Bake-Off." We brought each firm in and let them tell us why they should be paid 6% of total proceeds, as in, for every hundred million they'd raise in an IPO, they'd get $6 million cash off the top, plus all expenses paid and a boatload of other fees—all basically for pushing paper in front of potential investors. After bringing in what's called the "Elite 7," we chose to go with Credit Suisse. Two days after choosing them, they showed up with a team, all from Ivy League schools. They asked for a conference room and a copy machine and basically moved in, in prep for the big IPO.

They were shutting the rest of us out, and I was getting less confident they were acting in the interests of STI when I got a call from a lone wolf, but very smart lawyer who had turned investment banker. He'd heard we were going public and warned against the move, saying he had a billionaire that wanted to buy my company at a premium and I'd pay no fees to Credit Suisse in the sale. Turned off by the predatory tactics of Wall Street in general, I took the meeting with the billionaire; in less than twelve months, STI was his, and I was among the elites for real.

One of the very first things I did with the money from the sale was provide an endowment to Emory—the school that had given me so much—as well as Brenau, a small nonprofit college in Gainesville, Georgia.

I was determined to give kids growing up like I had a leg up. So many chances I'd been given were no longer there, and challenges I couldn't have imagined were now commonplace

The high school dropout rate in Georgia in 2004, the year I sold STI, was 6.5%, and the state's incarceration rate was among the highest in America.

My Brother Kenny

OVER TIME, I have struggled with my own addictions and a big one is that I work around the clock. However, while my addiction to work actually rewarded me once I left the swamp, things in some ways had been harder and more troubling for Kenny—but he had also married well and had two beautiful kids. After enlisting in the service following graduation, he served six years during which he married, had two children, and often mentioned how much he missed living on Swamp Road. His children, Casey and Lisa, would play a big part in my life. One example being when I got a divorce; both of them, by then college age, came and lived with me to help with my children, who both adored their older cousins.

Kenny had a genetic addiction issue like our granddaddy, Willie Oxford. A genetic heart disease called aortic stenosis also ran through our family, which I inherited. My heart murmur was diagnosed when I was thirteen and our family doctor, Porky Davis, referred us to a navy buddy of his named Dr. William Hurst. Dr. Hurst had been President Johnson's personal doctor in the White House and had become chief cardiologist of Emory. I got great care for a medical condition, but Kenny got quite the opposite.

Kenny could catch on faster to anything than the rest of us, but he also had what would be known now as Attention Deficit Disorder, which my son and I both struggle with, but not to the degree that Kenny did. Kenny had a nervous energy that was applied heavily to drinking and working; I could pick up pecans, crop tobacco, or plow with the tractor, but I was not in his league. But his frequent drinking rages and hell-raising kept him in trouble with Daddy, and Mary piled on the pain every chance she got. Instead of any kind of help for his addiction and ADD, he received harsh discipline from Daddy and emotional abuse from Mary.

But harsh discipline was quite common in the schools and homes in the Southern culture in the 1970s, and the lack of medical treatments for addiction and mental diseases are still present today. For that matter, with 116 hospitals closing in the very counties Trump carried by more than 60%, any medical care is getting very scarce in those communities. Before NAFTA, when you had a manufacturing and industrial base on those communities, the working class had health care benefits with insurance companies like Aetna paying the doctor and hospital bills. Without those companies, the citizens don't have the money, so the health care complexes also leave town, just like the jobs.

After his second tour with the Army, Kenny and his family moved back to Waycross, but Mary raised hell about them living in Grandmama's house and about Grandmama helping buy them milk and groceries. As Kenny struggled to find work in a declining wage and job environment, his drinking habit, which he'd had since high school, grew worse and worse. Grandmama, Beth, and I all helped his kids and wife, June, who he had met in Korea. She is extraordinarily people smart, poised, and wholeheartedly a good person. After Kenny's continued abuse of alcohol, she finally and desperately decided to take the kids to live with her sister in California. When he came home from a drinking binge to find his wife and children gone, it fell to me to explain that she had had no choice but take the kids and go.

Daddy gave him the old 1971 Pontiac and Kenny struck out for California. It solved two problems: 1) He could try to reunite with June and the kids, and 2) Mary finally got her wish of having Kenny gone. He turned up in California, sober and determined to get a job and make things right. There, he walked into Ralph's Grocery Store and was hired on the spot. Twenty years later, in February 2008, Kenny retired from that grocery store job and came home to Waycross—without his wife and family. In April, he drew his first pension check. But Waycross was becoming, literally, a ghost town. Most of the shops we knew were gone. Restaurants, too. Tebeau Street, which I used to think was beautiful, was a strip of abandoned buildings. Our dad was retired and living on Swamp Road with our stepmother. The railroad machine shop and cargo cleaning jobs were down to maybe a thousand slots. One of the companies that had been hiring for a while, Seven Out, on Francis Street, had shut down after a few years hauling and treating wastewater from industrial customers. The old gas and coke plant property, taken over by AGL, was a superfund site, as was the former railyard—two of a half dozen environmentally hazardous sites in Ware County. After Kenny returned home, I knew he had started drinking again. I also knew other people in town who were falling into harder addictions as the work, and the community around the work, dried up. And more and more, the people who remained were disenfranchised and poor and wandered through their lives on a meth high, an Oxy rush, or a bender.

But the country folk of Waycross and beyond saw a glimmer of hope in the form of a junior senator from Illinois. He pledged to put an end to the policies that had led to the Great Recession of that year, and to solve the high cost of health care. He called for more innovation in the form of technology and, subsequently, jobs. Perhaps most importantly, he was a Washington outlier by virtue of his race alone. He was a young man, speaking a populist message to a weary and dope-sick rural population who had turned out to vote for Barack Obama in numbers no one had seen in decades.

As the election returns came in proclaiming Obama the president in a landslide, my brother, who had been drinking heavily, was killed instantly in a single-car accident, not far from Swamp Road. That day, November 8, 2008, he had driven out to see my cousin Walter who lived out near a place called Pebble Hill, which had some sharp turns in the road called Dead Man Curves. With a bottle in a brown bag, Kenny ran off the road and flipped his truck; he passed away instantly, according to medical reports. Mary called and told me, "Kenny ran off the road and didn't make it," she said. I wish Daddy had called me, but Mary had always made all the decisions and blocked family communications.

When I realized what had happened, it hit me like a freight train. It was more than losing a brother; it made me realize that we had grown up in a fractured family, made worse by Mary. It hit me that my sister had done everything she could do to help Kenny. It hit me Kenny was leaving behind children, Casey and Lisa. It hit me how much our Grandmama would have been devastated by the news.

The She-Coon

UNCLE BUDDY WAS the husband of Mary's sister Alma who had come to live with us right after Daddy and Mary married, to escape the abuse of her father. She was not yet seventeen. Buddy was part of the Strickland family who lived a few houses down the road from us. Buddy had just graduated from high school and was working at basic jobs while waiting to be hired by the railroad. That job never came, so he opened his own carpet business. Buddy was gifted and talented.

Buddy was a Swamp Road ringleader in every good way and fortunately, he chose me at a young age to be his sidekick and confidante. Alma had what everybody considered were "Hollywood good looks." My Grandmother told Alma one time that she was the most beautiful woman she had ever met and Buddy had the hair and smile of Robert Redford. Both also were blessed with big smiles and personalities. They married when he was nineteen and Alma was a senior in high school, and they lived in a trailer next to his parents' house, right down the road from us.

Buddy had a huge impact on my life. He had excellent people skills and the only thing that held him back was his lack of expectations of ever leaving the swamp. But after I went off to college, Buddy was hired to be a plant manager and he rapidly moved up in the company and built a new house for his family.

For a couple of years, starting around age thirteen, I went coon hunting with Uncle Buddy. Because raccoons are nocturnal, we usually left for the woods at dusk and wouldn't return until the early morning hours, often with a bounty of one or two raccoons whose fur we sold for $10 to $15, depending on size and time of year.

Coon hunting as a sport requires a great deal of agility to be able to move and run with the dogs. We usually hunted with Buddy's dogs, Dan and Little Ann, who, along with other coonhounds—black and tans, blueticks, and walkers—had the natural proclivity to rush about and track in the creeks until they fell upon a fresh scent. Then their yelps would turn into steady barks to let us know they were on the coon's trail—and we were off to the races. As the dogs got hotter on the trail, their barks went from a longer tenor to a deep base, and Uncle Buddy would wave us into the swamp, and over and over yell out to the dogs, "speak to 'im," which sends a message to the dogs to stay on the coon trail and run the coon up a tree. As we waded into the water and joined in as a "speak to him" chorus, usually one of two things would happen: 1) The coon would fool the dogs and lose them by marking trees, running up one tree and hip scotching to others before running down one to safety, or 2) The dogs would get so close to the coon it would go up a tree for safety and be "treed" by the dogs, who would stand guard underneath. Hunters know when the coon is treed because the dogs have a specific treed voice, which is a deep long howl. At that point, Uncle Buddy would look at us and say, "treed," and we would take off through the woods for the kill.

Sometimes through the gator- and snake-infested swamps, we would cross chest-high water or trek as much as two or three miles to the tree. We hurried because the longer it took, the more time for the coon to jump to another tree and escape. We would shine our flashlights up into the tree until we spotted the coon, and then shoot it out of the tree and let it fight the snarling dogs—not quite dog fighting, but just as bad.

Coon hunting in South Georgia has all but disappeared, mainly for two reasons: Lack of jobs and an epidemic of obesity. Coon hunting was a sporting event that took money and energy. A skilled coon hunting hound that had the athletic skills to jump as high as eight feet in the air to clear the brush and was adept at three barks for tracking, trailing and treeing (yipping, barking, and howling, respectively) was known as a thousand-dollar dog because that's how much they cost. A newborn pup with papers (documented purity of lineage) or even a half-breed that could track and do a little trailing cost $250.

Along with waders, dogs, and flashlights, coon hunting requires a truck with a CB radio and a tankful of gas. You also need the right gun, the right shells, clothing, vests, and firewood made from fat lighter, the resinous wood of aged pine that burns raging hot like it was coated in lighter fluid.

Of course, the dogs had to be fed and came with medical bills, from snake bites to head wounds—it only takes a coon a few seconds to rip a dog's head wide open. I saw that happen one night. The dogs treed deep in the swamp—four or five miles away and water up to our waists. Uncle Buddy had on "waders"—rubbers boots that extended past your groin and around your waist and could cost (back then) between $26 and $75 depending on brand and contraptions. The rest of us were in regular Brogan boots and were soaked, head to toe, since we would invariably fall as we rushed to the tree. One night, to our surprise, the coon had come down the tree and was encircled by snarling dogs in the water. We shined our lights on it and saw the biggest she-coon we had ever seen—big as a sow pig—swimming toward the dogs. One by one, a dog would charge the coon, but before the others could race in, the she-coon would push the dog's head under water, rip the dog's face, and hurl it aside. Blood spurted from the dogs' ears, nose, and mouth and Uncle Buddy was trying to point the gun at the coon but could not get a clear shot without hitting one of the dogs. Uncle Buddy yelled, "She is going to kill these goddamn dogs!" He handed me the rifle and started walking toward the coon, carrying a big flashlight cocked behind his head. "If you get a good shot, shoot that son of a bitch," he yelled. About that time, Buddy grabbed his dog Dan by the collar and started to rally him in an encouraging voice, patting him on the side and then pushing him toward the coon saying, "sic him." Old Dan knew what this meant and tried, but the she-coon stood her ground and held his ears underwater and the dog nearly drowned until Uncle Buddy pulled him out by his hind legs. Uncle Buddy went toward the coon and hit it with his flashlight. The coon jumped at his legs, ready to rip them apart, but Uncle Buddy jumped to the other side of the tree. The coon was now chasing him around the tree and hissing. Donnie Cater, who was hunting with us, said, "I bet she has babies nearby." Uncle Buddy yelled at me to shoot, but I couldn't get a good shot. "Shoot him right now! This thing is going to kill me! Now dammit!" I yelled back, "I can't shoot—I'm afraid I might hit you."

By then, the she-coon was clawing Uncle Buddy's britches leg and he yelled, "Take a shot or give that gun to me." Finally, with the back side of the tree hiding the coon, she took off through the water toward dry ground. All the dogs were injured so Uncle Buddy took off after it and struck it on the head with his steel case flashlight. With the coon knocked unconscious, Uncle Buddy grabbed it by its tail and dragged it on land where we were all standing. He looked at me and said, "Shoot it in the head."

One day, I asked Uncle Buddy whether it was fair to shoot the coon out into a pack of six or seven dogs. He told me it would have been wrong to shoot the coon to kill it in the tree because it was up to us to give wildlife a sporting chance. Still today, I wish that, back then, we would have called the dogs off and led them back to the "dog boxes" in the bed of the pickup trucks and carried them to the next creek to hunt. But that would have been the equivalent of asking a teammate to score for the other team.

Lady Florence—the One That Got Away

HOW IN THE world did a redneck from Swamp Road get involved with elites? Admittedly, luck was on my side when I left the swamp. I worked for ten years at UPS, starting in the loading dock and working my way up to the corporate office. At UPS, I developed some critical technology for the company, that, in my first year there, saved it a quarter-million dollars. I was very well compensated in company stock from a global corporation. Besides my Uncle Waldo, who was safety director for the CSX Railroad, I was the first person in my family to wear a tie to work, and was surprised by the freedom that managerial and executive staffs had compared to that of blue-collar workers.

I also earned a Master of Business Administration (MBA) from Emory University, one of the more prestigious colleges in America. Emory was in Georgia, a half tank of gas from Swamp Road, but millions of miles difference in lifestyle. I was interacting with Ivy League students and professors, however, I was surprised at how little "smarts" factored into the equation of societal class structure. It was more about attitude and ambition, because the people in Waycross were just as smart.

With my MBA and UPS experience, I started STI Knowledge, a company that grew to offices in the US, the UK, South Africa, India, Hong Kong, and the Philippines and made the "Inc. 500" list of fastest-growing private companies in the US three years in a row, appearing as high as number thirteen on the list. After I Sold STI, I endowed MBA programs at Emory and Brenau University, and my elite credentials really soared when I began writing a column for the New York Times.

Emory held my endowment announcement at the ballroom of the Four Seasons in Atlanta. It was a long way from my silent, conditional acceptance, which was basically, "You're in, but don't tell anyone," all due to my undergraduate studies at West Georgia College. Emory prided and promoted itself on the brand association of having graduate students from the Ivy League. However, my endowment in millions of dollars, they were proud to proclaim—and welcomed my family from Waycross and hundreds of other friends and supporters of the university.

Emory was really the first time in my life where I had participated with so-called elites, and frankly, I learned a lot. At the ceremony was Zeke Burkawski, a board trustee for the

University of Monaco and whose wife, Dr. Dragana Burkawski, was in her final year of getting an MBA from Emory. After my endowment remarks, he asked me to speak at the university's MBA graduation ceremony, and a few days later, the dean of the school, Dr. Bill Lightfoot, called and asked if he could get a flight booked for me. I said yes, thinking that a paid trip to Monaco would be nice.

Monaco University overlooked the Mediterranean Sea and I opened my talk by saying they should all go into sales if they had talked their parents into paying for a Riviera Retreat. I noticed on-stage a very elegant and warm woman politely smiling while I was talking. I also noticed all the other faculty were giving her space and deference.

The university had invited Dr. Florence Eid, a high-profile finance professor from American University of Beirut, as a special guest of ceremonies. Florence personified elitism, but at the same time, was very warm and simple, with French-Lebanese beauty and smarts to match. Her next position was chief economist for Middle East North Africa (MENA), working with the elites in that region.

I saw Florence that evening at dinner and spent some time talking with her. Many of the others at the event were amazed that I was talking with Florence with such ease, since she was considered to be the most eligible woman in Lebanon. She had an education pedigree that included a handwritten note to Harvard letting them know she could not make it to freshman orientation because of a civil war blockade in her country. Harvard wrote back and said, basically: *Make it when you can. We understand.*

After dinner, I asked Florence if I could I walk her back to her hotel along the beautiful waterfront. She politely declined and said she was catching a cab, but offered to see me at breakfast the next morning where all the elites meet. I told her I would get there early and save her a place. The next morning, the men at breakfast asked me, "Is Lady Florence coming?" I proudly told them yes and that I was saving her a place; but she never showed, which was a tremendous letdown. She was the Jackie Kennedy I had always looked for.

I emailed her on my return to the US, letting her know that I wanted to see her again. After a couple of weeks, she responded with her phone number—of course, I picked up the phone and dialed right away. She was inviting me to speak at the American University of Beirut on the subject of entrepreneurship. I accepted and flew to Lebanon two short weeks later. I spoke at the university, and then spent days visiting cultural Arabic sights and learning long history lessons on European history. I think I finally won Florence over in two ways: Optimistic humor, which caused her to burst out in laughter, and: Cross knowledge—I could take her knowledge and cross reference to what I know, which meant that she was also learning from me.

After a period of time, we set a wedding date in Atlanta. But that was disrupted with a deadline on her tenure track because she was leaving the university to go into private enterprise. I told her we could get married anytime, but she had one shot at tenure so I told her to stay and work.

We were together six wonderful years, but never married. But it was the flood of memories roaring in my head about the agony of a fractured family that kept us from considering marriage earlier. People often ask me why I have still not remarried after eighteen years. Lady Florence was the one who got away. The rest of the road hasn't been without its hurdles either. I have had some bad breaks—a bitter divorce, an on-and-off Democrat in a deep red state, and a planned TV show that was cancelled at the last minute.

The swamper comes out in me because Idon't quit. I later created and ran the Oxford Center for Entrepreneurs and the daily publication, *Morning Report*, before selling both in 2018. In 2004, I ran in a field of fourteen candidates for the United States Senate. I lost the race, but in the process got an inside look at the Washington, DC campaign fundraising machine. In my disappointment with both parties, and probably more so with Democrats, I am now an Independent. In the 2018 election, I voted for Republican Brian Kemp for governor and my last campaign contribution was to Bernie Sanders, not because I was voting for him, but because I do think he is the most honest person from either party on the national stage. Yet, for the 2020 presidential election, I remain undecided—I'm somewhere between the elites and the "deplorables." With my redneck roots, I will never be fully accepted by the elites. And although Swamp Road is in my blood, I have no immediate plans to return there.

ENDNOTES

THE END OF THE BEGINNING

1   Palmer, Shane Goldmacher and Doug, Louis Nelson, and Nick Gass. "Gingrich Reverses Course on Trade as Trump VP Chatter Swirls," July 1, 2016. https://www.politico.com/story/2016/07/newt-gingrich-trum p-trade-vice-president-225035.

2   Kessler, Glenn. "Analysis | The Strange Tale about Why Bill Clinton Said NAFTA Would Create 1 Million Jobs." The Washington Post. WP Company, September 21, 2018. https://www.washingtonpost.com/ politics/2018/09/21/strange-tale-about-why-bill-clinton-said-nafta-would-create-million-jobs.

3   Ibid

4   Ibid

CHAPTER 1 | You Don't Know Me, But You Don't Like Me

1   Food Service Associate Salary in Waycross, GA. Accessed August 17, 2020. https://www.indeed.com/salaries/food-service-associate-Salaries,-Waycross-GA.

CHAPTER 2 | Killin' Time

1   Kessler, Glenn. "Analysis | The Strange Tale about Why Bill Clinton Said NAFTA Would Create 1 Million Jobs." The Washington Post. WP Company, September 21, 2018. https://www.washingtonpost.com/ politics/2018/09/21/strange-tale-about-why-bill-clinton-said-nafta-would-create-million-jobs.

2   U.S. Bureau of Labor Statistics, Current Employment Statistics survey, series ID CES3000000001, manufacturing industry, U.S. Department of Labor, extracted Feb. 6, 2018. Available at: http:// www.bls.gov/ces/.

3   Abusaid, Shaddi. "South Georgia Newspaper Publisher Found Dead in Office." ajc. The Atlanta Journal-Constitution, October 23, 2019.

https://www.ajc.com/news/crime--law/south-georgia-newspape r-publisher-found-dead-office/RKP0B61UjhbRYlAkcv2ZfK/.

4   Rich, Frank, Alex Carp, and Tony Millionaire. "The Trump Voters Who Don't Deserve Democrats' Sympathy." Intelligencer, March 20, 2017. https://nymag.com/intelligencer/2017/03/ frank-rich-no-sympathy-for-the-hillbilly.html.

5   "The Decline of the White Working Class: St. Louis Fed." The Decline of the White Working Class | St. Louis Fed. Accessed August 17, 2020. https://www.stlouisfed.org/household-financial-stability/ the-demographics-of-wealth/decline-of-white-working-class.

6   Worst-Online-Dater. "Tinder Experiments II: Guys, Unless You Are Really Hot You Are Probably Better off Not Wasting Your..." Medium. Medium, March 25, 2015. https://medium.com/@worstonlinedater/ tinder-experiments-ii-guys-unless-you-are-really-hot-you-are-p robably-better-off-not-wasting-your-2ddf370a6e9a.

7   Giese, Rachel. "The Epidemic of Isolation Among Young Men." The Walrus, August 22, 2019. https://thewalrus.ca/the-epidemic-of-isolatio n-among-young-men/.

CHAPTER 3 | Loving Swamp and Holding Elites

1   Glass, Andrew. "Reagan Fires 11,000 Striking Air Traffic Controllers, Aug. 5, 1981." POLITICO, August 5, 2017. https://www.politico.com/ story/2017/08/05/reagan-fires-11-000-striking-air-traffic-controll ers-aug-5-1981-241252.

2   Bartash, Jeffry. "Share of Union Workers in the U.S. Falls to a Record Low in 2019," January 31, 2020. https://www.marketwatch. com/story/share-of-union-workers-in-the-us-falls-to-a-record-l ow-in-2019-2020-01-22.

3   Porter, Eduardo. "Ross Perot's Warning of a 'Giant Sucking Sound' on Nafta Echoes Today." The New York Times. The New York Times, July 9, 2019. https://www.nytimes.com/2019/07/09/business/economy/ ross-perot-nafta-trade.html.

4   Carnes, Nicholas, and Noam Lupu. "Why Trump's Appeal Is Wider than You Might Think." MSNBC. NBCUniversal News Group, April

8, 2016. http://www.msnbc.com/msnbc/why-trumps-appeal-wider-yo
u-might-think.

5   Nunberg, Geoff. "A Resurgence Of 'Redneck' Pride, Marked By Race, Class And Trump." A Resurgence Of 'Redneck' Pride, Marked By Race, Class And Trump | WBUR News. WBUR, September 6, 2016. https://www.wbur.org/npr/492183406/a-resurgence-of-redneck-prid e-marked-by-race-class-and-trump.

6   Juliana Menasce Horowitz, Ruth Igielnik and Rakesh Kochhar. "Trends in U.S. Income and Wealth Inequality." Pew Research Center's Social & Demographic Trends Project, May 27, 2020. https://www.pewsocialtrends.org/2020/01/09/trends-in-income- and-wealth-inequality/.

7   Ibid.

8   http://www.census.gov/hhes/www/income/data/historical/families.

9   Juliana Menasce Horowitz, Ruth Igielnik and Rakesh Kochhar. "Trends in U.S. Income and Wealth Inequality." Pew Research Center's Social & Demographic Trends Project, May 27, 2020. https:// www.pewsocialtrends.org/2020/01/09/trends-in-income-and- wealth-inequality/.

10 "Social Explorer Tables: ACS 2017 (5-Year Estimates) (267 Tables) - Social Explorer Tables: ACS 2017 (5-Year Estimates) (SE) - ACS 2017 (5-Year Estimates)." Social Explorer. Accessed August 17, 2020. https:// www.socialexplorer.com/data/ACS2017_5yr/metadata/?ds=SE.

**CHAPTER 4 | Country Sunshine—"Livin'
Like We Used To" Before the Coup**

1   Azarian, Bobby. "A Complete Psychological Analysis of Trump's Support." Psychology Today. Sussex Publishers, December 27, 2018. https:// www.psychologytoday.com/us/blog/mind-in-the-machine/201812/ complete-psychological-analysis-trumps-support.

CHAPTER 5 | Mile Marker 1: When Push Comes to Shove—The PATCO Strike

1   Collins, Michael, Maureen Groppe, and Ledyard King. "Fed-up Workers, Repairs Delayed, Missed Mortgage Payments: Why the Government Shutdown Never Ended for Some." USA Today. Gannett Satellite Information Network, July 27, 2019. https://www.usatoday.com/story/news/politics/2019/07/27/government-shutdown-lingering-effects-reverberate-six-months-later/1807287001/.

2   Common Dreams, and Jon Queally. "TSA Strike? As Trump and GOP Refuse to End Shutdown, Call Grows for Federal Workers to Rise Up." Common Dreams, January 14, 2019. https://www.commondreams.org/news/2019/01/14/tsa-strike-trump-and-gop-refuse-end-shutdown-call-grows-federal-workers-rise.

3   Schalch, Kathleen. "1981 Strike Leaves Legacy for American Workers." NPR. NPR, August 3, 2006. https://www.npr.org/2006/08/03/5604656/1981-strike-leaves-legacy-for-american-workers.

4   http://dollarsandsense.org/archives/1981/1081patco.html.

5   https://www.ssa.gov/oact/cola/AWI.htm.

6   Planes, Alex. "The Day Ronald Reagan Disarmed the American Labor Movement." The Motley Fool. The Motley Fool, August 5, 2013. https://www.fool.com/investing/general/2013/08/05/the-day-ronald-reagan-weakened-the-american-labor.aspx.

7   Common Dreams, and Michael Moore. "30 Years Ago: The Day the Middle Class Died." Common Dreams, August 6, 2011. https://www.commondreams.org/views/2011/08/06/30-years-ago-day-middle-class-died?utm_campaign=shareaholic.

8   Hrynowski, Zach. "What Percentage of U.S. Workers Are Union Members?" Gallup.com. Gallup, April 8, 2020. https://news.gallup.com/poll/265958/percentage-workers-union-members.aspx.

9   https://www.bls.gov/opub/mlr/1983/02/art1full.pdf.

10 https://www.bls.gov/opub/mlr/1990/09/Art1full.pdf.

11 Report • By Robert E. Scott • August 11. "Manufacturing Job Loss: Trade, Not Productivity, Is the Culprit." Economic Policy Institute.

Accessed August 17, 2020. https://www.epi.org/publication/manufacturing-job-loss-trade-not-productivity-is-the-culprit/.

12 Morin, Richard. "AMERICA'S MIDDLE-CLASS MELTDOWN." The Washington Post. WP Company, December 1, 1991. https://www.washingtonpost.com/archive/opinions/1991/12/01/americas-middle-class-meltdown/5ed5f8b6-d9ac-4282-b3d8-166cf2c1e80a/.

13 Ibid.

CHAPTER 6 | Mile Marker 2: Give It Away—NAFTA

1 Bureau, US Census. "Computer and Internet Use in the United States: 1984 to 2009." The United States Census Bureau, August 8, 2016. https://www.census.gov/data/tables/time-series/demo/computer-internet/computer-use-1984-2009.html.

2 https://fred.stlouisfed.org/series/GAWARE9URN.

3 Cillizza, Chris. "Ross Perot 2012! His Message Was 20 Years Ahead of Its Time." The Washington Post. WP Company, July 20, 2012. https://www.washingtonpost.com/opinions/ross-perot-2012-his-message-was-20-years-ahead-of-its-time/2012/07/20/gJQAazGeyW_story.html.

4 The Associated Press. "'Giant Sucking Sound': Perot's Quips Over the Years." U.S. News & World Report. U.S. News & World Report. Accessed August 17, 2020. https://www.usnews.com/news/business/articles/2019-07-09/giant-sucking-sound-perots-quips-over-the-years.

5 https://en.wikipedia.org/wiki/Ross Perot.

6 Waxman, Olivia B. "Who Started NAFTA and Why? What to Know as Trump Moves On." Time. Time, November 30, 2018. https://time.com/5468175/nafta-history/.

7 "When Wal-Mart Went to Mexico." Harvard University Press Blog. Accessed August 17, 2020. https://harvardpress.typepad.com/hup_publicity/2012/04/wal-mart-in-mexico-bethany-moreton.html.

8 Auerbach, Stuart, and Edward Cody. "BOOM OVER THE BORDER: U.S. FIRMS GO TO MEXICO." The Washington Post. WP Company, May 17, 1992. https://www.washingtonpost.com/

archive/politics/1992/05/17/boom-over-the-border-us-firms-g
o-to-mexico/9ca6eb93-76cb-47fa-86d8-ecc5630059e8/.

9 Dislocated Workers: An Early Look at the NAFTA Transitional
Adjustment Assistance Program. Accessed August 17, 2020. https://
www.govinfo.gov/content/pkg/GAOREPORTS-HEHS-95-31/html/
GAOREPORTS-HEHS-95-31.htm.

10 https://www.piie.com/publications/chapters preview/3802/
10iie3802.pdf.

11 Jackson, Robert. "Clinton Sees NAFTA Gains, Urges Foes to Dismiss
Fears." Los Angeles Times. Los Angeles Times, November 14, 1993.
https://www.latimes.com/archives/la-xpm-1993-11-14-mn-56962-
story.html.

12 https://en.wikipedia.org/wiki/North American Free Trade
Agreement

13 "NAFTA's Impact on U.S. Workers." Economic Policy Institute. Accessed
August 17, 2020. https://www.epi.org/blog/naftas-impact-workers/.

14 NAFTA job retraining program out of money. Accessed August 17,
2020. https://nwlaborpress.org/2001/4-20-01NAFTA.html.

15 "NAFTA's Impact on U.S. Workers." Economic Policy Institute. Accessed
August 17, 2020. https://www.epi.org/blog/naftas-impact-workers/.

16 Darlington, Shasta, and Patrick Gillespie. "Mexican Farmer's Daughter:
NAFTA Destroyed Us." CNNMoney. Cable News Network. Accessed
August 17, 2020. https://money.cnn.com/2017/02/09/news/economy/
nafta-farming-mexico-us-corn-jobs/index.html.

17 Parsons, Cameron. "NAFTA and the Environment in Mexico."
Modern Latin America. Accessed August 17, 2020. https://
library.brown.edu/create/modernlatinamerica/chapters/chapte
r-12-strategies-for-economic-developmen/nafta-free-trade-and-th
e-environment-in-mexico/.

18 "History of American Sweatshops: 1940-1997." National Museum of
American History. Accessed August 17, 2020. https://americanhistory.
si.edu/sweatshops/history-1940-1997.

19 Palmer, Shane Goldmacher and Doug, Louis Nelson, and
Nick Gass. "Gingrich Reverses Course on Trade as Trump
VP Chatter Swirls." POLITICO, July 1, 2016. https://www.

politico.com/story/2016/07/newt-gingrich-trump-trade-vice-president-225035.

20 Faux, Jeff. "NAFTA's Impact on U.S. Workers." Economic Policy Institute, December 9, 2013. https://www.epi.org/blog/naftas-impact-workers/.

21 Bebar, Jill. "Wall St. Ends Record Year." CNNMoney. Cable News Network, December 31, 1999. https://money.cnn.com/1999/12/31/markets/markets_newyork/.

22 https://www.investopedia.com/terms/g/gatt.asp

CHAPTER 7 | Mile Marker 3: Misery Loves Company—The Opioid Addiction Crisis

1 Levin, D. (2020, February 23). Teaching Children How to Reverse an Overdose. Retrieved August 17, 2020, from https://www.nytimes.com/2020/02/23/us/opioids-tennessee-narcan-training.html?referringSource=articleShare.

2 https://www.cdc.gov/drugoverdose/maps/rxcounty2018.html.

3 Ibid

4 Timeline | The Meth Epidemic | FRONTLINE. (2006, February 14). Retrieved August 17, 2020, from https://www.pbs.org/wgbh/pages/frontline/meth/etc/cron.html.

5 History.com Editors. (2017, June 7). History of Meth. Retrieved August 17, 2020, from https://www.history.com/.amp/topics/crime/history-of-meth.

6 Patterson, E. (2018, December 04). Meth Facts, History and Statistics: Dangers and Legality. Retrieved August 17, 2020, from https://drugabuse.com/methamphetamine/history-statistics/.

7 Timeline | The Meth Epidemic | FRONTLINE. (2006, February 14). Retrieved August 17, 2020, from https://www.pbs.org/wgbh/pages/frontline/meth/etc/cron.html.

8 Engle, J. (2013, August 12). Who's blocking this astonishingly effective tool to fight meth labs? Retrieved August 17, 2020, from https://www.motherjones.com/politics/2013/08/meth-pseudoephedrine-big-pharma-lobby/.

9 History.com Editors. (2017, June 07). History of Meth. Retrieved August 17, 2020, from https://www.history.com/topics/crime/history-of-meth.

10   Crystal Methamphetamine Use Statistics - The Meth Epidemic - Drug-Free World. (n.d.). Retrieved August 17, 2020, from https://www.drugfreeworld.org/drugfacts/crystalmeth/a-worldwide-epidemic-of-addiction.html.

11   Reinberg, Steven. Meth Use, Addiction on the Rise Among Americans: CDC. (n.d.). Retrieved August 17, 2020, from https://www.usnews.com/news/health-news/articles/2020-03-26/meth-use-addiction-on-the-rise-among-americans-cdc.

12   History of Crystal Meth Addiction. (n.d.). Retrieved August 17, 2020, from https://www.michaelshouse.com/crystal-meth-addiction/history/.

13   Allen, G. (spring 2019). Pushing opioids for profits. *International Socialist Review,* (112). doi:https://isreview.org/issue/112/pushing-opioids-profits.

14   Ryan, Harriet, Lisa Girion, and Scott Glover. "'You Want a Description of Hell?' OxyContin's 12-Hour Problem #InvestigatingOxy." Los Angeles Times. Los Angeles Times, May 5, 2016. https://www.latimes.com/projects/oxycontin-part1/.

15   Van Zee, A. (2009, February). The promotion and marketing of oxycontin: Commercial triumph, public health tragedy. Retrieved August 17, 2020, from https://www.ncbi.nlm.nih.gov/pmc/articles/PMC2622774/.

16   Keyes, K. M., Phd, Cerdá, M., DrPh, Brady, J. E., SM, Havens, J. R., PhD, & Galea, S., MD, DrPH. (2014, February). Understanding the Rural–Urban Differences in Nonmedical Prescription Opioid Use and Abuse in the United States. Retrieved August 17, 2020, from https://www.ncbi.nlm.nih.gov/pmc/articles/PMC3935688/.

17   Ryan, H., Girion, L., & Glover, S. "Inside an L.A. OxyContin Ring That Pushed More than 1 Million Pills. What the Drugmaker Knew." Los Angeles Times. Los Angeles Times, July 10, 2016. https://www.latimes.com/investigation/la-me-pharma-day-two-20160701-snap-story.html.

18   Whitaker, Bill. "Did the FDA Ignite the Opioid Epidemic?," February 24, 2019. https://www.cbsnews.com/news/opioid-epidemic-did-the-fda-ignite-the-crisis-60-minutes/.

19 Bigg, Matthew. "Nine-Year-Olds Plotted to Tie up, Hurt Teacher." Reuters. Thomson Reuters, April 2, 2008. https://www.reuters.com/article/us-school-plot-idUSN0126796220080402.

20 "States with the Highest Unemployment Rates, April 2009." U.S. Bureau of Labor Statistics. U.S. Bureau of Labor Statistics, May 27, 2009. https://www.bls.gov/opub/ted/2009/may/wk4/art02.htm?view_full.

21 "Unemployment Rate in Ware County, GA." FRED, July 29, 2020. https://fred.stlouisfed.org/series/GAWARE9URN.

22 The Daily Beast. "Tiny West Virginia Town Flooded With 3 Million Opioids During Drug Epidemic." The Daily Beast. The Daily Beast Company, December 20, 2018. https://www.thedailybeast.com/tiny-west-virginia-town-flooded-with-3-million-opioids-during-drug-epidemic.

23 Gutierrez, Gabe, Adam Reiss, and Corky Siemaszko. "Welcome to Williamson, W.Va., Where There Are 6,500 Opioid Pills per Person." NBCNews.com. NBCUniversal News Group, February 2, 2018. https://www.nbcnews.com/news/us-news/welcome-williamson-w-va-where-there-are-6-500-opioid-n843821.

24 Basu, Tanya. "How OxyContin Kicked Off the Heroin Epidemic." The Daily Beast. The Daily Beast Company, April 12, 2018. https://www.thedailybeast.com/how-oxycontin-kicked-off-the-heroin-epidemic.

25 "Increases in Drug and Opioid Overdose Deaths - United States, 2000–2014." Centers for Disease Control and Prevention. Centers for Disease Control and Prevention. Accessed August 17, 2020. https://www.cdc.gov/mmwr/preview/mmwrhtml/mm6450a3.htm.

26 https://www.congress.gov/bill/114th-congress/senate-bill/483.

27 Higham, Scott, and Lenny Bernstein. "Did President Obama Know Bill Would Strip DEA of Power?" The Washington Post. WP Company, October 16, 2017. https://www.washingtonpost.com/investigations/did-president-obama-know-bill-would-strip-dea-of-power/2017/10/15/86fe711c-b03a-11e7-9e58-e6288544af98_story.html.

28 Ibid.

29 Morrell, Alex. "The OxyContin Clan: The $14 Billion Newcomer to Forbes 2015 List of Richest U.S. Families." Forbes. Forbes Magazine, March 24, 2016.

https://www.forbes.com/sites/alexmorrell/2015/07/01/the-oxycontin-cla n-the-14-billion-newcomer-to-forbes-2015-list-of-richest-u-s-families/.

30 Meier, Barry. "In Guilty Plea, OxyContin Maker to Pay $600 Million." The New York Times. The New York Times, May 10, 2007. https:// www.nytimes.com/2007/05/10/business/11drug-web.html.

31 Armstrong, David. "OxyContin Maker Explored Expansion Into 'Attractive' Anti-Addiction Market." ProPublica. Accessed August 17, 2020. https://www.propublica.org/article/oxycontin-purdue-pharm a-massachusetts-lawsuit-anti-addiction-market.

32 https://www.mass.gov/doc/massachusetts-7/download.

33 Ibid.

34 Geller, Adam. "NY Finds $1B in Hidden Transfers by Family behind OxyContin." AP NEWS. Associated Press, September 14, 2019. https:// apnews.com/81039e579ad74a8db531124b362c9b86.

35 Merle, Renae. "Judge in Purdue Pharma Bankruptcy Case Extends Lawsuit Protection to Sacklers." The Washington Post. WP Company, November 6, 2019. https://www.washingtonpost.com/business/2019/11/06/judg e-purdue-pharma-bankruptcy-extends-lawsuit-protection-sacklers/.

36 https://www.merriam-webster.com/dictionary/premeditated.

CHAPTER 8 | Finger Lickin' Bad—Southern Fare to Fast Food

1 Anzilotti, Eillie. "Why Dollar Stores Are Bad Business for the Neighborhoods They Open In." Fast Company. Fast Company, December 18, 2018. https://www.fastcompany.com/90278384/wh y-dollar-stores-are-bad-business-for-the-neighborhoods-they-open-in.

2 Prabhu, Maya T. "Food Stamp Use Is Highest in Rural Georgia. So Are Grocery Prices." ajc. The Atlanta Journal-Constitution, November 27, 2019. https://www.ajc.com/news/state--regional-govt- -politics/georgia-food-stamp-use-and-prices-run-highest-rural-areas/ 7RNmDJUynvycInEwfEGH1J/.

3 Ibid

4 Ibid

5 Ibid.

6   Swaminathan, Aarthi. "'It's Really Troubling': Parts of America Are Trapped in a 'Catch-22' Economic Situation." Yahoo! Finance. Yahoo!, July 1, 2019. https://finance.yahoo.com/news/rural-america-distresse d-communities-181618799.html.

7   Cranley, Ellen. "Diet Coke, McDonald's, and Meatloaf: These Are Trump's Favorite Foods." Business Insider. Business Insider, July 1, 2019. https://www.businessinsider.com/donald-trump-favorite-food s-steak-cake-diet-coke-2019-7.

8   "Why Good Nutrition Is Important: Center for Science in the Public Interest." Why Good Nutrition is Important | Center for Science in the Public Interest. Accessed August 17, 2020. https://cspinet.org/ eating-healthy/why-good-nutrition-important.

9   Darby, Luke. "72 Percent of All Rural Hospital Closures Are in States That Rejected the Medicaid Expansion." GQ. GQ, July 30, 2019. https://www.gq.com/story/rural-hospitals-closing-in-red-states.

10   Williams, Joseph P. "Working as a Doctor in Rural America Is a 'Different Reality'." U.S. News & World Report. U.S. News & World Report, August 22, 2018. https://www.usnews.com/news/healthiest-communities/ articles/2018-08-22/rural-doctor-shortage-a-drag-on-community-health.

11   Saslow, Eli. "'Urgent Needs from Head to Toe': This Clinic Had Two Days to Fix a Lifetime of Needs." The Washington Post. WP Company, June 22, 2019. https://www.washingtonpost.com/national/ the-clinic-of-last-resort/2019/06/22/2833c8a0-92cc-11e9-aadb-74e6b2b46f6a_story.html.

12   Schaefer, Anna. "What Causes Mountain Dew Mouth?" Healthline. Healthline Media, February 25, 2015. https://www.healthline.com/ health/dental-and-oral-health/mountain-dew-mouth.

13   McCann, Adam. "States with the Most and Least Student Debt." WalletHub, July 10, 2019. https://wallethub.com/edu/e/best-and-wors t-states-for-student-debt/7520/.

CHAPTER 9 | Rhinestone Elites

1   108 Marchese, David. "Jon Stewart Is Back to Weigh In." The New York Times. The New York Times, June 15, 2020. https://www.nytimes.

com/interactive/2020/06/15/magazine/jon-stewart-interview.html. *(A guest on "The Daily Show" in 2014 while she was House minority leader. The back-and-forth that Stewart describes here is his paraphrasing of the conversation.)*

2   Lendman, Stephen. "'The True Story of the Bilderberg Group' and What They May Be Planning Now." Global Research, May 28, 2019. https://www.globalresearch.ca/the-true-story-of-the-bilderberg-group -and-what-they-may-be-planning-now/13808.

3   https://bilderbergmeetings.org/index.html.

4   "Ronald Reagan." SAG. Accessed August 17, 2020. https://www. sagaftra.org/ronald-reagan.

5   Kirkpatrick, David D. "How a Chase Bank Chairman Helped the Deposed Shah of Iran Enter the U.S." The New York Times. The New York Times. Accessed August 17, 2020. https://www.nytimes. com/2019/12/29/world/middleeast/shah-iran-chase-papers.html.

6   Ibid.

7   https://clinton.presidentiallibraries.us/items/show/36014.

8   Klazema, Michael. "Top 10 Largest Employers in the USA." backgroundchecks.com, November 21, 2018. https://www. backgroundchecks.com/community/Post/5836/Top-10-Larges t-Employers-in-the-USA.

9   "Author Joel Stein on Sticking up for the 'Intellectual Elite'." PBS. Public Broadcasting Service, November 14, 2019. https://www.pbs.org/newshour/ show/author-joel-stein-on-sticking-up-for-the-intellectual-elite.

CHAPTER 10 | Desperado

1   Bishop, Bill, and Tim Murphy. "Obama Closes Gap in Rural Vote, Wins Bigger in Cities." Daily Yonder, July 17, 2019. https://dailyyonder.com/ obama-closes-gap-rural-vote-wins-bigger-cities/.

2   Bishop, Bill. "One More Time: Rural Voters Didn't Desert Dems in 2008." Daily Yonder, May 31, 2018. https://dailyyonder.com/one-tim e-rural-voters-didnt-desert-dems-2008/2018/05/31/.

3   Davey, Monica, Bill Vlasic, and Mary Williams Walsh. "Detroit Ruling on Bankruptcy Lifts Pension Protections." The New York Times.

The New York Times, December 3, 2013. https://www.nytimes. com/2013/12/04/us/detroit-bankruptcy-ruling.html.

4   Whoriskey, Peter. "He's 79 and Working Full Time at Walmart: A Sobering Truth for Those without Pensions." sacbee. The Sacramento Bee. Accessed August 17, 2020. https://www.sacbee.com/latest-news/ article191519519.html.

5   Sabelhaus, John, and Alice Henriques Volz. "Board of Governors of the Federal Reserve System." The Fed - Are Disappearing Employer Pensions Contributing to Rising Wealth Inequality?, February 1, 2019. https://www.federalreserve.gov/econres/notes/feds-notes/ar e-disappearing-employer-pensions-contributing-to-rising-wealt h-inequality-20190201.htm.

6   Berkes, Howard. "Retiring on the Edge of Poverty in Rural America." NPR. NPR, April 14, 2006. https://www.npr.org/templates/story/story. php?storyId=5342818.

7   Jaffe, Susan, West LA, Shaw D, Verhaegh KJ, Baldwin T, Et Al., Cecil G, and Harrell R. "Aging In Rural America." Health Affairs, January 1, 2015. https://www.healthaffairs.org/doi/full/10.1377/ hlthaff.2014.1372.

8   Gabriel, Trip. "When Health Law Isn't Enough, the Desperate Line Up at Tents." The New York Times. The New York Times, July 23, 2017. https://www.nytimes.com/2017/07/23/us/healthcare-uninsured-rura l-poor-affordable-care-act-republicans.html.

9   Oppel, Richard A., and Kristine Potter. "'A Cesspool of a Dungeon': The Surging Population in Rural Jails." The New York Times. The New York Times, December 13, 2019. https://www.nytimes.com/2019/12/13/us/ rural-jails.html.

10 Rose, Steve. "The Forgotten Man: a Fitting Oil Painting for Trump's America." The Guardian. Guardian News and Media, November 17, 2016. https://www.theguardian.com/artanddesign/2016/nov/17/jo n-mcnaughton-painting-trump-white-house-the-forgotten-man.

11 https://www.census.gov/quickfacts/waycrosscitygeorgia.

12 Sharpe, Joshua, and Reisigl, Joe. "Why Are so Many People Getting Rare Cancers in This Small Georgia Town?" Atlanta Magazine, April

24, 2019. https://www.atlantamagazine.com/great-reads/why-are-rar
e-cancers-killing-so-many-people-in-a-small-georgia-town/.

13   "Long-Term Trends in Deaths of Despair." - United States Joint Economic
Committee, September 5, 2019. https://www.jec.senate.gov/public/
index.cfm/republicans/2019/9/long-term-trends-in-deaths-of-despair.

CHAPTER 11 | From Rhetoric to Reverie

1   Frizell, Sam. "Hillary Clinton Transcript: Read Full Text of Clinton
Campaign Launch." Time. Time, June 13, 2015. https://time.
com/3920332/transcript-full-text-hillary-clinton-campaign-launch/.

2   Sanders, Sen. Bernie. "Remarks by Sen. Bernie Sanders." The Burlington
Free Press, May 27, 2015. https://www.burlingtonfreepress.com/story/
news/2015/05/26/remarks-by-sen-bernie-sanders/27979493/.

3   Carroll, Lauren. "PolitiFact - Hillary Clinton's Top 10 Campaign
Promises." POLITICO, July 22, 2016. https://www.politifact.com/
article/2016/jul/22/hillary-clintons-top-10-campaign-promises/.

4   Vogel, Kenneth P. "Pro-Sanders Super PAC Brought in $2.3 Million."
POLITICO, January 31, 2016. https://www.politico.com/story/2016/01/
bernie-sanders-super-pac-218478.

5   Terrell, Anthony. "Trump Out-Campaigned Clinton by 50 Percent
in Key Battleground States in Final Stretch." NBCNews.com.
NBCUniversal News Group, February 8, 2017. https://www.nbcnews.
com/politics/2016-election/trump-out-campaigned-clinton-50-perc
ent-key-battlegrounds-final-100-n683116.

6   Roberts, Timmons. "Trump's Case against Free Trade Makes No
Sense." Newsweek, May 28, 2016. https://www.newsweek.com/
trump-globalization-free-trade-tariff-immigration-undocume
nted-expulsion-436101.

7   Visser, Nick. "Head Of CBS Says Trump Is 'Damn Good' For
Business." HuffPost. HuffPost, September 6, 2018. https://www.
huffpost.com/entry/les-moonves-donald-trump_n_56d52ce8e4
b03260bf780275?guccounter=1.

8   Boehlert, Written by Eric. "ABC World News Tonight Has Devoted
Less Than One Minute To Bernie Sanders' Campaign This Year."

Media Matters for America. Accessed August 17, 2020. https://www. mediamatters.org/abc/abc-world-news-tonight-has-devoted-les s-one-minute-bernie-sanders-campaign-year.

9   Byler, David. "Poll Position: Where Clinton, Trump Stand on Election Eve." RealClearPolitics, November 7, 2016. https://www.realclearpolitics. com/articles/2016/11/07/poll_position_where_clinton_trump_stand_ on_election_eve_132270.html.

10   Kahn, Mattie. "All Across the Nation, Women Wore Pantsuits to Vote for Hillary." ELLE. ELLE, October 9, 2017. https://www.elle.com/ fashion/personal-style/news/g29092/pantsuit-nation-women-wea r-pantsuits-to-vote-for-hillary/.

11   Kaufman, Gena. "Enjoy These Photos of Adorable, Patriotic Kids in Pantsuits." ELLE. ELLE, November 8, 2016. https://www.elle. com/culture/news/gmp29088/enjoy-these-photos-of-adorabl e-patriotic-kids-in-pantsuits/.

12   Blevins, Joe. "Thousands Are Planning to Point and Laugh at Trump Tower Tomorrow." News. News, August 23, 2017. https://news. avclub.com/thousands-are-planning-to-point-and-laugh-at-trump- towe-1798254050.

13   "2016 Presidential General Election Results - Ware County, GA." Dave Leip's Atlas of U.S. Presidential Elections - State Data. Accessed August 17, 2020. https://uselectionatlas.org/RESULTS/statesub. php?year=2016.

14   Soffen, Kim, Samuel Granados, Ted Millnik, and John Muyskens. "Two Swing States Show Why Clinton Lost." The Washington Post. WP Company, November 9, 2016. https://www.washingtonpost.com/ graphics/politics/2016-election/precinct-results/.

15   File, Thom. "Voting in America: A Look at the 2016 Presidential Election." The United States Census Bureau, May 10, 2017. https:// www.census.gov/newsroom/blogs/random-samplings/2017/05/ voting_in_america.html.

16   McElwee, Sean. "Why the Voting Gap Matters." Demos, October 23, 2014. https://www.demos.org/research/why-voting-gap-matters.

Dad (Willie Clyde), my older brother, Kenny, and me

Back row, from left: My sister Beth, me, my brother, Kenny
Front row, from left: Matt and my grandmother

After working all day outside in the July sun. From left to right: my cousin Walter (Aunt Shirley's oldest son), Grandmama, and my brother, Kenny.

Dad's brother—my uncle Kenny—who bought approximately about 47.3 acres of land for Grandmama with his combat pay in WWII.

House where we lived with dad and grandparents. Grandaddy is on front porch.

Grandmother with sisters Loudel, Adel, and Edna

Speaking at Porsche in Stuttgart, Germany and Florence joining from Lebanon.

CPSIA information can be obtained
at www.ICGtesting.com
Printed in the USA
LVHW080418131020
668649LV00009B/337